KT-437-294

GOOD LIVING AT CHRISTMAS

WITH *Jane Asher*

GOOD LIVING AT CHRISTMAS

WITH *Jane Asher*

CREATIVE IDEAS FOR YOUR FAMILY AND HOME

BBC

This book has been published to accompany the TV series *Good Living*, a BBC Manchester production.

Series Producer: Ben Frow
Producer: Emma Westcott

Published by
BBC Worldwide Ltd, Woodlands,
80 Wood Lane, London W12 0TT

First published in 1998

(For a full list of contributors and photographers see page 127)

ISBN 0 563 38463 8

Art directed by Ellen Wheeler

Designed by Janet James

Printed and bound in Great Britain
by Butler & Tanner Ltd, Frome & London
Colour separations by Radstock Reproductions Ltd, Midsomer Norton
Jacket printed by Lawrence Allen Limited, Weston-super-Mare

Much of the material in this book has previously been published in *Good Living with Jane Asher*, a supplement to BBC *Good Food Magazine*.

contents

introduction

Christmas has always been one of my favourite times of year – not only because of the celebrations and festivities, but because it's the holiday when the whole family tends to gather together.

The secret of enjoying it is to plan ahead as much as possible, get as many things done before the great day as you possibly can, then relax and not worry about those things you haven't managed to do.

It's great fun and much more satisfying to make your own decorations, cards, cakes and presents, but Christmas is such a busy time of year that I'm all for cheating as much as necessary to make it easier to cope. There's no point in struggling to do everything yourself if it means you're going to end up too stressed and exhausted to enjoy yourself.

Good Living at Christmas is about ideas and inspirations to make your Christmas special without the panic and pressure. All the craft and food ideas are simple and economical yet impressive, and you can easily adapt them according to how much time you have to spare. There are gorgeous decorations to make your home look really magical, unusual ideas for easy hand-made cards and wrapping paper, edible presents that make perfect gifts for just about anyone, elegant menus for festive entertaining and recipes for spectacular Christmas cakes. I think you'll find there's something for everyone.

I hope you will have as much fun trying out these ideas as I have – they'll certainly make Christmas that little bit more special and less frantic.

Have a very happy Christmas!

Jane Asher

JANE ASHER

CHAPTER ONE

decorations

Christmas just wouldn't be the same without the decorations that give your home that really festive feeling, both inside and out. Making decorations is great fun and forms part of the festivities – and the rest of the family will love joining in too.

I've got some great ideas here for you to make your home look really magical this Christmas – and, best of all, they are all quick and easy to make.

tree *decorations*

Here are two very different but equally beautiful trees. The first, the orange cookie tree, uses ingredients almost entirely from the kitchen for the decorations. Inspired by Hansel and Gretel, this cookie-laden tree will particularly delight the children with its fairytale feel.

The purple and silver tree has a glamour and magic all of its own. But, like the cookie tree, the decorations are quick and easy to make and cost next to nothing.

Orange ring

All citrus fruits can be sliced and dried for 4–6 hours in a very cool oven. When cold, tie on to the tree with raffia.

Orange and cinnamon pendants

Tie a knot at the end of a piece of string, thread on kumquats, a ribbon bow, cinnamon sticks and a dried orange slice (see above), then make a loop in the string to hang on the tree. (Kumquats look beautiful but only last for a few days; tie on hazelnuts or almonds for a longer lasting display.)

Pomanders

Stud a double row of cloves around a clementine and tie narrow ribbon between the rows. Stud two single rows, to divide the clementine into quarters, and tie to the tree with a bow. This decoration should last the 12 days of Christmas.

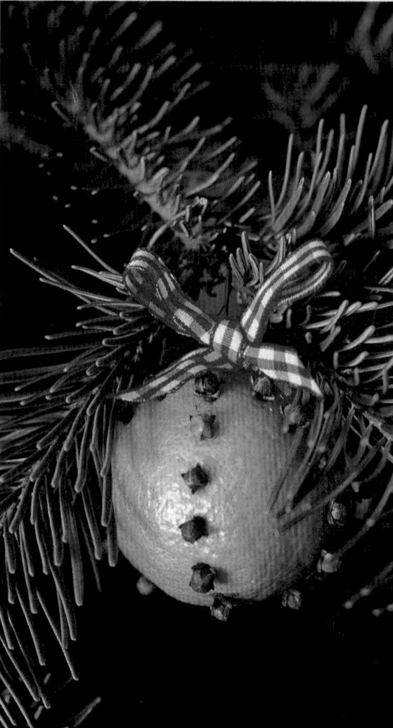

Cellophane twists

Pop sweets into a 15cm/6in square of amber cellophane, twist to close, then tie to the tree with raffia.

Cranberry ring

Using fine florist's wire, thread on up to 20 dried cranberries. Twist the wire ends together and trim. Tie to the tree with raffia.

Christmas tree biscuits

Once baked (see page 120 for templates), decorate with piped royal icing and silver dragées. When dry, tie to the tree with narrow ribbon.

Makes about 30

200g/7oz self-raising flour
115g/4oz light muscovado sugar
100g/3½ oz butter, at room temperature
1 tbsp ground ginger
½ tsp salt
1 egg
packet royal icing, dragées, thin ribbon and golden caster sugar, to decorate

1 Place all the biscuit ingredients in a food processor and mix together to form a dough, then knead briefly on a lightly floured surface. Cut the dough in half, wrap in plastic film and chill for 1 hour or until firm.

2 Preheat the oven to 180°C/350°F/Gas 4. Roll out half the dough at a time on a lightly floured surface to 5mm/¼ in thick. Cut out shapes from card using the templates (see page 120): place on top of the dough, then cut round using a small sharp knife. Lift with a small palette knife on to an ungreased baking tray. If they become mis-shapen, push back into shape.

3 Using the blunt end of a wooden skewer, make a hole at the top of each biscuit, so you can later thread with ribbon for hanging on the tree. (For the double heart biscuit decoration, shown right, make a hole at both the top and bottom of the larger heart.) Bake in batches for about 8 minutes, or until just beginning to turn brown around the edges. If the holes have filled in during baking, widen them again with the skewer while the biscuits are still warm. Leave the biscuits on the baking tray for a few minutes to firm before moving to a wire rack to cool.

4 Decorate the biscuits with icing and dragées as shown in the photographs.

5 Finally, when dry, tie to the tree with colourful narrow ribbon.

Foil plaques

Cut out two 7 x 5cm/3 x 2in pieces modelling foil. On the reverse side of one, draw the frame using a soft pencil, then draw a motif, such as a Christmas tree, freehand. Stick the pieces, wrong sides together, with wide double-sided tape, sandwiching a piece of hanging wire between them. Thread a clear bead on to the wire, then shape the wire into a hook to hang on the tree. Finally, tie on a silver ribbon.

Net bags

Cut a 20cm/8in square of star-studded net (plain white net will be fine if you cannot find star-patterned net). Fill with sugar almonds or silver dragées, tie into a bundle with fine wire and twist the ends into a hook to hang on the tree. Decorate with a silver ribbon ringlet.

Floating feather

Wire up the quill end of the feather with a small piece of fine florist's wire and hook on the tree.

Paper moon

This is simply made using white blotting paper and the template on page 121. Trace the template on to card and cut out. Place this on the blotting paper and paint the outline on to the paper using water and a fine brush, then carefully tear around the outline. Tie a piece of fine wire around the top of the moon, thread on a single bead, then shape the wire into a hook to hang on the tree.

Crystal drops

Thread a variety of different shaped clear and silver beads on to fine florists' wire to make these little gems. Shape a hook at the end to hang on the tree.

Foil leaves

Using the templates on page 121, cut out several leaves in modelling foil. On the reverse, mark on the leaf detail using a soft pencil, then wire up in pairs to hang on the tree.

Beaded heart

Using fine florist's wire, thread on 25 clear glass beads. Twist wire ends together and trim. Shape into a heart, and add a wire hook to the top of the heart.

Icicle cones

Using the template on page 121, cut out the cone in silver wrapping paper. Twist to form a cone, overlapping at the top by 2cm/¾in, then secure on the inside with tape. Pierce two holes at the top of the cone, one on either side, thread with silver cord and knot to secure. Fill with sweets.

Christmas is the perfect excuse to dress the house in a way that would be over the top at any other time of year. All these decoration ideas can be adapted to a shelf or even a window sill, which would not only look lovely inside your home, but would also create a dramatic effect from outside for all to see.

WARNING Take care that decorations are not placed too close to candles or fire, and that you do not use candles on a shelf if there is another shelf immediately above. Always extinguish the candles before you leave the room. For all these ideas, electric Christmas lights can used instead of candles for safety.

mantelpiece *ideas*

Children's fireplace

1 Fasten colourful baubles and other brightly painted hanging decorations to the mantelpiece.

2 Stack the top with teddy bears, other cuddlies, wooden toys and parcels.

3 Finally don't forget to hang the stockings, to either side of the mantelpiece.

Golden glow

1 Cover the mantelpiece with ivy and dot with gold ornaments, candles, Christmas cards, bundles of cinnamon sticks tied with gold ribbon, dried poppy seed heads sprayed gold, and fruit (satsumas, kumquats and cape gooseberries, for example) tied with gold and tartan ribbon.

2 Add a gold box and a gold carrier bag filled with tissue paper and topped with fruit.

3 The clove-studded clementine on page 10 or the oranges shown on page 27 would also look stunning here.

Tinsel town

1 Make a star with three wire coat hangers, secured at each join with fine fuse wire. Remove hooks with pliers and twist tinsel around the wire hangers to cover them entirely. Secure to the wall with a picture hook.

2 Intertwine Christmas tree lights with tinsel and loop under the mantelpiece, securing with insulating tape.

3 Arrange brightly wrapped presents on the top, accessorized with candlesticks and ornaments.

Silver sophistication

1 Create a magical mood with a mantelpiece adorned with silverware, ribbons, tissue paper and boxes filled with chocolates and sweets.

2 Entwine with twigs, draped plastic fruit, and leaves and nuts sprayed with silver paint.

3 The simple white candles and flowers complete this elegant display.

You needn't go out and buy lots of decorations for your home. All the ideas here are very simple yet so pretty and natural looking, and many of them use materials that most of us have around the home. They can be made in moments, cost next to nothing and some of them can also be made by the younger and most excited members of the family.

decorations around *the home*

Lavender stars

These make perfect gifts and can decorate your home all year. Cut five twigs to an equal length then, using fine florist's wire, attach dried lavender sprigs along their length. Wire the twigs together to make a star. Also perfect for the top of the tree.

Signed and sealed

Make your party invitations stand out by sealing the envelope with gold cord and sealing wax stamped with your family initial.

Bubbling baubles

Select your favourite large bowl and fill to overflowing with co-ordinating coloured baubles. It's so easy but looks extremely effective.

Chair decorations

Add a special touch to your dining room by decorating the chairs. Make several small posies with seasonal foliage, secure with ribbon, then tie with a bow to the back of each chair. To preserve, remove before sitting down.

WARNING **Don't forget that ivy and some berries are poisonous, so keep out of children's reach.**

Leaf garland

A foil leaf garland twisted through a stem of plain green ivy sets a fireplace off to perfection. Follow the instructions on page 16 to make the foil leaves, then wire them on to a fine tinsel rope before intertwining with the ivy. Attach the garland to the fireplace with adhesive putty. You could also drape the leaf garland around picture frames.

Clove-studded oranges

Stud oranges with cloves spelling out the word 'XMAS' and pile up in a bowl with other oranges and evergreen twigs.

Door tags *(right)*

If you have a houseful this Christmas, allocate the rooms and welcome your guests with a pretty posy of ivy and berries tied with a ribbon and name tag to their bedroom doors. This idea, with a welcome tag, also makes a refreshing alternative to a traditional front door wreath.

Oyster shell candles *(left)*

These are easy to make and the same shells can be refilled to make new candles. Plug any holes in the shell with plasticine. Melt down two white household candles (enough for six shells) and retrieve the wicks with tweezers, taking care not to get hot wax on your skin. Allow the wax to cool slightly, then pour into the first shell. Dip in the end of the wick and hold straight. When the wax has set (about 5 minutes), trim the wick to 1cm/½in and repeat the process with the remaining shells. Display together on a plate surrounded by ivy and red berries.

Twig wreath *(left)*

This can be made in minutes. Take a ready-made twig circle bought from a garden centre, and loosely wind the ivy trails around it, securing with florist's wire. Tie on small bunches of red berries.

Window dressing

Let winter sunshine add sparkle to your windows by stitching crystal tree ornaments or beads to the edges of your curtains. Drape some ivy over the curtain rail and down the curtain to finish.

A few special touches will make all the difference to your table when you are entertaining, and the simple elegance of these decorations will really set the scene for a special supper. All the table decoration ideas here can be made in a matter of seconds, cost very little and, most important, look lovely.

Place-name cards *(right)*

These tiny cards can be written well in advance, then trimmed with a sprig of foliage just before your guests arrive. Simple fold a small rectangle of heavy white card in half – the cards stand horizontally on their longer edge. Write your guests' names in gold or silver pen.

Menu planning *(far right)*

One of the easiest ways to cope with Christmas at home, especially if you are doing a lot of entertaining, is to plan meals well in advance. Impress your family and guests by leaving menus on a tray for anyone to read during the day. Write the menus with a metallic gold or silver pen on heavy white paper. Roll the menus up and tie with soft furnishing tassles.

table *decorations*

Candlestick trims *(right)*

Transform plain candlesticks by tying delicately coloured organza ribbon in a simple bow around the stems of each one. Here, contrasting colour ribbons and candles have been used, but this decoration would be just as effective with matching coloured candles and ribbon.

Party bundles *(far right)*

Decorate your table with these pretty candle bundles, which can double up as gifts for your guests. Small silver candles are tied with silver ribbon and trimmed with rosemary and tiny golden baubles. You could even add a foil name tag (see page 54) to each one, to double up as a place name and a gift tag.

JANE

Ivy place names

What could be simpler for place names than writing on a leaf? All you need is a green leaf for each place setting, such as ivy or holly, and a metallic silver or gold pen to write your guests' names.

Painted glass

Give plain glass a festive look by decorating it with white acrylic paint. Use a fine brush and paint the outside of the bowl of the glass below the lip line. At the end of the evening the decoration can be easily washed away.

Napkin rings naturally

Add a fragrant twist to your Christmas table by decorating crisp, white napkins with delicate stems of rosemary and ivy.

Individual menus

Make a Christmas dinner party extra special by placing a handwritten menu between each pair of guests. It's also a great way to get them talking.

medieval *table decorations*

A touch of medieval richness on the Christmas table makes a glorious centre-piece for the family gathering. Any richly patterned, medieval-style paper will look good for covering the crown and napkin ring.

Napkin rings

Follow the method for the crown on page 34. Cover a 15 x 6cm/6 x 2½ in piece of card with medieval-style wrapping paper. Cut a 2cm/¾ in deep, narrow zigzag pattern along one of the long sides. Join the narrow ends with sticky tape and tie a tassel around the middle.

'Noel' place cards

Cut a piece of 20 x 15cm/8 x 6in card and fold in half widthways. Cut parchment paper the same width and 5cm/2in longer, then scroll each end by curling around a pencil. With the folded edge of the card at the top, stick the paper to the front of the card with the scrolled ends at the top and bottom. Cut a decorative 'N' from the medieval-style wrapping paper, or trace one from a copyright-free source book of medieval calligraphy and colour it in yourself. Stick the letter on to the front of the card. Pencil in the outline for the remaining letters in medieval-style script, then use a gold felt-tip pen to fill the letters in. You can write your guests' names underneath in gold pen, or substitute 'Noel' with their names if you prefer.

Medieval crowns

Cut a 46 x 13cm/18 x 5in piece of medieval-style wrapping paper and stick to a piece of card the same size. Along the length of one side, cut an even zigzag pattern 5cm/2in in depth, to make the points of the crown. With the paper facing out, join the two narrow ends of the card with sticky tape, and finish with a Christmas decoration looped over one of the crown points. Fill the crown with fabric or tissue paper (you could also hide a small gift inside) and drop gold covered chocolate coins on top.

Frosted grape display

Dip a bunch of grapes into beaten egg white, then sprinkle with caster sugar to create a frosted look.
Place in a bowl with satsumas sprayed with gold paint for a truly lavish display. Decorate with an ivy sprig also sprayed gold.

Peacock feather napkin rings

This impressive alternative to napkin rings is so simple to make. For each napkin, take a 20cm/8in length of wired ribbon and cut an inverted v-shape at each end to neaten. Tie this round your folded napkin and tuck the peacock feather under it.

It is very satisfying to make your own crackers. These are so much more original and fun than any you could buy in a shop, and you can easily incorporate your own themes and ideas. Why not try and make crackers in colours to co-ordinate with your table linen and crockery? Friends and family will be really excited to have a personalized cracker with their own very special gift inside.

If you don't want to make them from scratch, you can easily use cheap ready-made ones. Just gently open one end to pop a present in, then re-cover and decorate them however you want.

beautiful crackers

YOU WILL NEED

37 x 16cm/14½ x 5¼in piece of decorative paper • **11 x 14cm/4¼ x 5½in piece of white paper** • 1 snap, gift, motto and hat • **3 cardboard tubes 11cm/4¼in long x 4cm/1½in diameter – toilet roll centres are ideal** • clear drying adhesive • **string** • scissors and a pin to perforate the paper • **decorative ribbons, fabrics and trims**

Making a basic cracker

All the crackers on the following pages use the basic cracker.

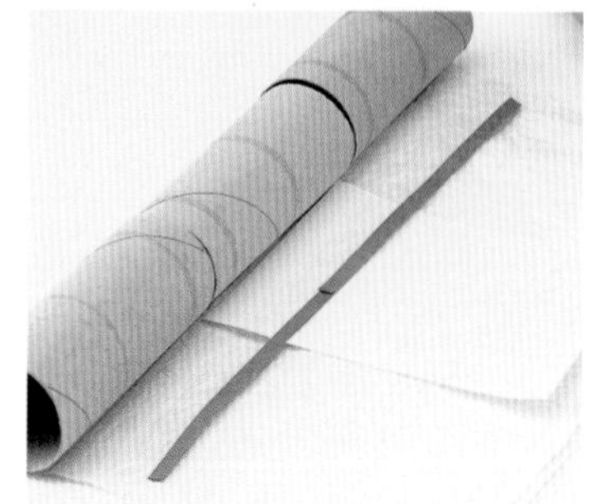

1 Place the decorative paper right side down, position the white paper on top so it will encircle the middle roll, then the snap and the three cardboard rolls side by side. Spread adhesive along the lower edge of the decorative paper.

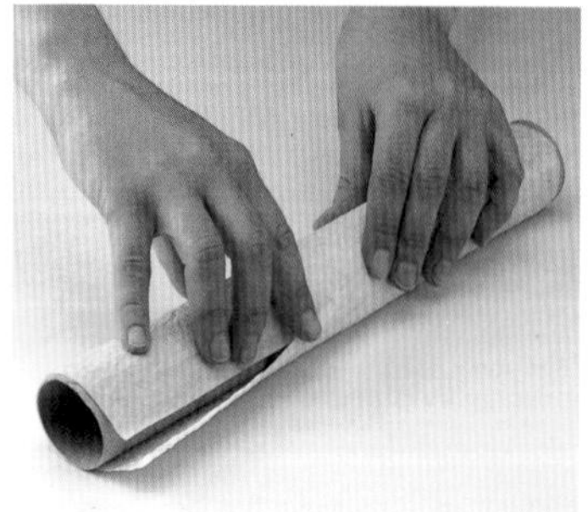

2 Hold the tubes together and roll up the papers around them, pressing along the edge to secure. Separate the tubes leaving a 4cm/1½in gap between them. It's a good idea to leave all the tubes in place while you decorate the crackers.

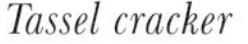

Tassel cracker

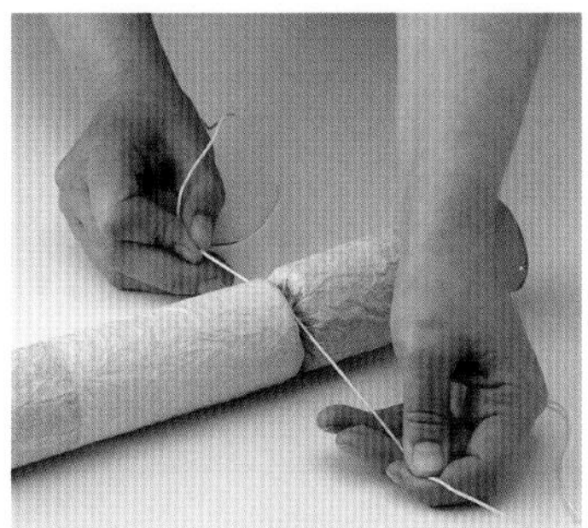

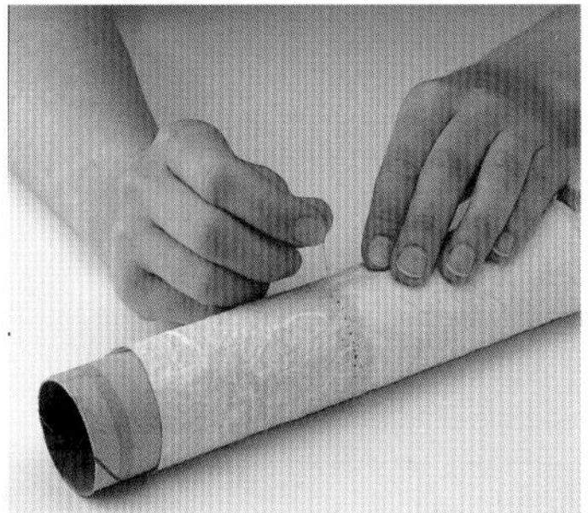

3 Shape one end of the cracker by wrapping string around the gap between the tubes. Gently pull the ends to gather up the paper, then unwind the string.

4 Pop a personalized gift (remember to label the crackers), motto and hat into the ungathered end of the cracker. If you want to pull the cracker easily, use a pin to make a ring of perforations in the paper between the tubes, then gather as before. Once the crackers are complete, remove the two end tubes.

Tassel cracker *(illustrated on page 37)*

YOU WILL NEED

2 x 5cm/2in long furnishing tassels • **thread** • 1m/40in length of 5cm/2in wide voile ribbon • **clear adhesive** • 1 evergreen stem, fresh or silk

1 Tie each tassel to the cracker ends with thread.

2 Cut the ribbon in half and tie into a bow at each end of the cracker. Finish by sticking the evergreen stem in place.

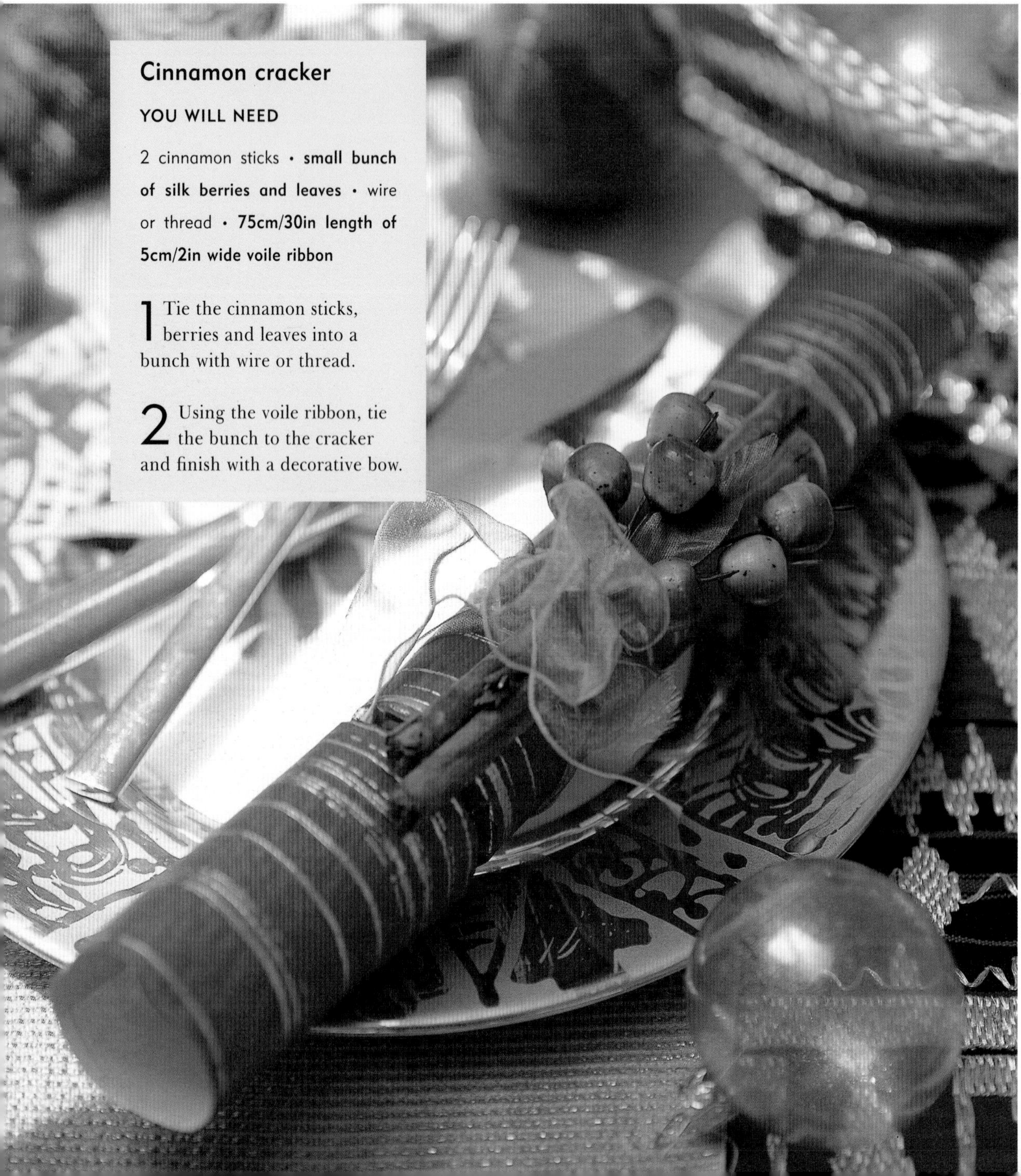

Cinnamon cracker

YOU WILL NEED

2 cinnamon sticks • **small bunch of silk berries and leaves** • wire or thread • **75cm/30in length of 5cm/2in wide voile ribbon**

1 Tie the cinnamon sticks, berries and leaves into a bunch with wire or thread.

2 Using the voile ribbon, tie the bunch to the cracker and finish with a decorative bow.

Wacky gem cracker

YOU WILL NEED

clear adhesive • **multi-coloured craft gems** • 30 x 35cm/ 12 x 14in piece of netting • **matching sewing thread** • 1m/40in tubular braid • **fine garden wire**

1 Stick the gems in a scattered design over the basic cracker. Loosely wrap the net around and tie in place over the shaped ends with matching thread.

2 Cut the tubular braid into two equal lengths and thread the fine garden wire down the centre of each. Wind the wired braid around a pencil to create a spiral shape, then twist the braid around each cracker end to secure.

Golden cracker

YOU WILL NEED

needle • **thread** • 2 strips 15 x 46cm/6 x 18in gold-star netting • **gold spray paint** • dried leaves • **empty snail or sea shells** • clear adhesive

1 Make a row of running stitches, lengthways, down the centre of each strip of net. Gather up the net and tie in place around the shaped ends of the cracker.

2 Spray paint the leaves and shells, then stick in place.

Turquoise cracker

YOU WILL NEED

30 x 16cm/12 x 6¼in piece of coloured, creased paper • **string** • silver embroidery thread • **needle** • 2 strips 15 x 46cm/6 x 18in matching netting • **silver spray paint** • dried seed pods from the garden or five-star anise pods • **clear adhesive**

1 Wrap the creased paper around the basic cracker and, using the string as before, shape the ends.

2 Using the silver thread, make a row of running stitches, lengthways, down the centre of each strip of net. Gather up the net and tie in place around the shaped ends of the cracker, carefully securing the creased paper in place at the same time.

3 Spray paint the seed pods and stick in place. Finish by winding silver thread around the cracker ends.

Galaxy cracker

YOU WILL NEED

clear adhesive • **stars** • 75cm/30in length of 6cm/2½in wide ribbon

1 Stick the stars in a scattered design over the galaxy cracker.

2 Tie the ribbon in a generous bow at one end of the cracker.

Tartan cracker

YOU WILL NEED

1m/40in length of 5cm/2in wide tartan ribbon • **1 ivy stem – fresh or silk** • clear adhesive

1 Cut the ribbon in half and tie into a bow at each end of the cracker. Snip the ribbon ends in an inverted 'V' shape as shown, to neaten.

2 Twist the stem of ivy around the cracker and secure on the underside with clear adhesive.

WARNING **Fresh ivy is poisonous, so do not give these crackers to children and, for safety, avoid using fresh, possibly poisonous berries on crackers. Be careful, too, with fresh evergreens.**

There is nothing like a Christmas wreath to get you and your seasonal visitors into the Christmas spirit. This one, using variegated ivy found in the garden, could not be simpler to assemble and would look stunning inside or outside the house. The lovely holly ball on page 45 could not be easier to make and looks just as effective as a wreath. For a fun alternative which the children will adore, we have also made a version of the holly ball using brightly coloured sweets.

the holly and *the ivy*

Kumquat and monkey-nut wreath

YOU WILL NEED

30cm/12in diameter fresh flower florist's foam ring • **stems of plain ivy** • 10 – 15cm/4 – 6in lengths of variegated ivy • **15cm/6in lengths strong florist's wire – about 80** • 9 kumquats • **9 gold poppy head cups (ready-bought)** • 26 decorative dried flower seed heads or star anise • **6 small fir cones** • 8 gold poppy seed heads (ready bought) • **6 monkey nuts** • 1m x 2cm/40 x ¾in wide checked ribbon

1 **Preparing the ring** Immerse the foam ring in water for about 20 minutes to soften the foam.

2 **Creating the foliage outline and ivy twist** Set the size and style of the wreath by pushing short stems of the plain ivy into the ring to fill it completely. Fold the lengths of florist's wire in half to make a hairpin shape and use to pin lengths of the variegated ivy across sections of the wreath on a diagonal, to give the impression that the ivy twists round the wreath. Everything added after the foliage will be placed within this basic framework.

3 Kumquat groups Pin groups of three kumquats around the ring, equally spaced, using the hairpin-shaped florist's wire. Then do the same for the gold poppy head cups, pinning them in threes evenly in the spaces between the kumquats.

4 Filling in the wreath Fill in the rest of the wreath with the dried flower seed heads or star anise, small fir cones, the poppy seed heads and the monkey nuts, fixing them in place with the hairpin-shaped florist's wire.

5 Finishing touches Tie a bow with the ribbon and pin it to the bottom of the wreath with florist's wire.

Sweet bombe

YOU WILL NEED

foam florist's ball • **metal skewer for hanging** • 2.25kg/5lb sweets in assorted colour wrappers • **15cm/6in lengths strong florist's wire – about 50** • 2m x 3cm/2½yd x 1¼in wide purple ribbon (or more if you are hanging the ball high up)

1 Push the skewer through the ball until it appears at the other side. Bend the end with pliers to secure. You will need this for hanging the ball as it is very heavy. The loop of the skewer is the top end of the ball.

2 Wire together a cluster of three sweets on lengths of florist's wire, folded in half to make a hairpin shape. Push these clusters into the foam ball to cover it entirely.

3 Finish with ribbons as for step 3 of the holly ball. Tie the length of ribbon for hanging the ball through the top loop of the metal skewer.

Holly ball

YOU WILL NEED

foam florist's ball • **holly, a large carrier bag full, cut into 5cm/2in stems** • plastic holly berries – about 20 (optional) • **2m x 3cm/2½yd x 1¼in wide purple ribbon (or more if hanging the ball high up)** • 15cm/6in lengths strong florist's wire – about 2 • metal skewer for hanging

1 Immerse the ball in water for about 20 minutes to soften the foam.

2 Set the size and style of the ball by pushing holly stems of the same length into the ball. Position them around the ball evenly to keep the circular shape. Continue until the entire ball is covered. If your holly does not have lots of natural berries, or if you have children, add plastic ones, poking them into the foam ball evenly in between the holly.

3 Cut off 75cm/30in of the ribbon, tie a bow and pin to the top of the ball with a length of florist's wire, folded in half to make a hairpin shape. Cut another 75cm/30in for the tails – snip the ends of the ribbon into an inverted v-shape, then simply fold the ribbon in half and pin at the fold to the underside of the ball with a piece of wire. Use the remaining ribbon to hang the ball – if you want to hang it from somewhere high up, such as a ceiling, you will need more ribbon. Push a skewer into the top of the ball. Thread the ribbon through the loop of the skewer then tie the ends into a knot. Hang the ribbon loop from a nail or screw.

CHAPTER TWO

cards & gifts

Christmas is the time of giving, and it's fun to make some presents yourself. I have included some sparkling ideas for gifts, and for home-made cards, gift-wrap and gift-tags.

The edible gifts are a real treat – ideal for the difficult-to-buy-for, and perfect for the foodies in your family. Friends and family will feel extra-special knowing that you have gone to the effort of making something for them, yet all these ideas are simplicity itself.

Hand-made cards mean so much more than bought ones, but you may have been put off in the past by the thought of them being too difficult or time-consuming. Well, think again – these cards are simplicity itself to make, and they look so original. They will certainly stand out from the crowd on your friends' and families' mantelpieces!

hand-made *cards*

Christmas present card

YOU WILL NEED

20cm/8in square of red card • **8cm/3¼in square of gold wrapping paper** • sticky tape • **30cm/12in length of 1cm/½in wide tartan ribbon, trimmed in an inverted v-shape at the ends to neaten** • glue

1 Fold the card in half. Place the gold paper face down, and fold the corners back to make a smaller square. Secure with sticky tape.

2 Face up, tie the ribbon round the square as though tying it round a present, and finish with a bow. Stick on to the card with glue.

Red Christmas tree card

YOU WILL NEED

17 x 25cm/6½ x 10in rectangle of red textured paper • **60cm/24in length of fine fuse wire** • sticky tape

1 Fold the red paper in half. Cut a 1cm/½in piece from the fuse wire and put on the side. Fold the rest of the fuse wire in half, then fold in half again. The point of the fold forms the top point of the star.

2 Using tweezers, bend one side of the wire to make the points of one side of a small star, then repeat on the other side.

3 Twist the wire at the bottom of the star and then fashion the tree shape and tub in the same way. When complete, twist the ends of the wire tightly at the base to secure.

4 Hook the short length of wire around the top of the star, twist lightly and poke through the front of the card. On the reverse side, fold the wire down and secure with sticky tape.

Leaf card *(not illustrated)*

YOU WILL NEED

tree leaves, such as oak • **22 x 37cm/ 8½ x 14½in square heavy gold card** • glue

1 Press leaves in a heavy book for two weeks or until dry.

2 Fold the card in half. Glue a dried leaf to the front of the card.

Christmas pudding card

YOU WILL NEED

13 x 22cm/5 x 8½in rectangle of heavy white card • **dark red, brown and green paper** • glue • **chopping board** • sharp craft knife

1 Measure where the card will fold lengthways and mark lightly in pencil.

2 Cut a small oval plate out of the red paper and glue along the fold line.

3 Cut pudding, holly and berry shapes from brown, green and red paper, respectively. Glue into position on the card as shown.

4 Place the card on to the chopping board and, using the sharp craft knife, cut around the top of the pudding, around the holly and the top of the plate, down to the fold line only.

5 Fold the card along the pencil line, pushing the pudding out from behind so that it pops up.

Green and gold Christmas tree card

YOU WILL NEED

18 x 29cm/7 x 11½in rectangle of green corrugated card • **13 x 8cm/5 x 3¼in piece of gold paper** • red paper • **glue**

1 Fold the green card exactly in half. Stick the gold paper rectangle to the front of the card in the centre.

2 Draw a Christmas tree shape freehand on a piece of red paper, cut out carefully, then glue on to the gold paper in the centre.

Purple star card

YOU WILL NEED

18cm/7in square of purple card • **46cm/18in length of fine fuse wire** • sticky tape

1 Fold the purple card in half. Following the instructions for the Red Christmas tree card (see page 49), make a star shape out of the fine fuse wire, but this time use up all the wire to make a bigger star.

2 Join the wire at the top to complete the star and twist the remaining wire round and round repeatedly at the top leaving enough to hook over the card.

3 Make a hook at the end to hang over the top of the card and affix to the inside back of the card with sticky tape.

Star anise card *(opposite)*

YOU WILL NEED

13 x 28cm/5 x 11in rectangle of natural-coloured corrugated paper • **7.5 x 5cm/3 x 2in rectangle of gold paper, torn out roughly** • glue • **2 star anise pods (available in the spices section of most supermarkets)** • gold spray paint • **a stem of fresh ivy** • gold glitter

1 Fold the corrugated paper in half. The card stands on its shorter edge, with the fold at the top.

2 Glue the gold paper rectangle to the card in the centre.

3 Place the star anise on newspaper and spray with gold paint. Take a stem of fresh ivy, dot the leaves with glue and sprinkle with gold glitter.

4 Glue the ivy stem diagonally across the card from one corner to the other, and then glue the star anise on either side, on the opposite corners of the gold paper.

Holly-pattern fabric card *(above)*

YOU WILL NEED

22 x 37cm/8½ x 14½in rectangle of heavy green card • **17cm/6½in square of calico** • red fabric paint or fabric pen • **fabric glue**

1 Fold the green card in half. Fray the edges of the calico slightly.

2 Draw a pattern of tiny holly leaves 2 – 3cm/ ¾ – 1¼ in from the edge of the calico using the fabric paint or pens, and write a message in the centre. Glue on to the card.

TIPS

- Card sizes are flexible; buy envelopes before making your card, then cut the cards to fit the size of your envelopes.
- Use a gold or silver marker pen to write a greeting inside your cards.
- Use fabric glue when adhering fabric or other non-paper items. For paper, use clear drying adhesive.
- Spray paints, fabric paints and pens, glitter and adhesives are available from all good art and craft shops. Ribbon, calico and fabric glue from department stores or haberdashers. Fuse wire is available from electrical and DIY stores.

Wreath card *(right)*

YOU WILL NEED

20cm/8in square heavy white card • **glue** • gold glitter • **fine black pen** • gold cord

1 Fold the white card in half. The card stands horizontally, on its longer edge.

2 In the centre of the front of the card, make a wreath shape with the glue, then dust with gold glitter.

3 When dry, write your festive message around the wreath using a fine black pen, and tie the cord round the fold of the card.

Sometimes wrapping presents can seem like a real chore. I often leave it to the last minute, and my wrapping ends up being rushed and looking boring. But this year, I'm determined to try these lovely, simple ideas. None of them takes long to make, but friends and family will really appreciate you taking that little extra trouble to make their gifts look special.

It would be a pity to spoil your beautiful hand-made gift wrap with obviously shop-bought tags, so here are a couple of inventive and very pretty designs that will complement all the gift-wrap ideas on the following pages.

Cookie gift tags

Make the cookie tags using the dough recipe on page 12 and the tree template on page 120 for the shape. Then, using a sharp knife, carefully cut out the appropriate initial from the centre of the cookie and make a hole in the top for the ribbon before baking.

Tin-foil tags

These are made from two 4 x 6cm/1½ x 2in pieces of modelling foil stuck together with wide double-sided tape. Emboss the name and design on the wrong side using a soft pencil – remember to write the name back to front! Punch a hole for the ribbon and tie to a gift.

gift wrap *& tags*

Chloe

See instructions on next page for making the gift-wrap ideas illustrated here.

String of stars

Make a paper chain of shiny stars to brighten a plain parcel. Cut a 2cm/¾in wide strip of red paper, and fold at 2.5cm/1in intervals, like a concertina. Draw a five-pointed star on the top piece with the top point of the star on one fold and the two lower points of the star on the other. Cut out, taking care not to cut the folded edges. Open out and wrap around the parcel, securing with glue or sticky tape.

Lavender blue

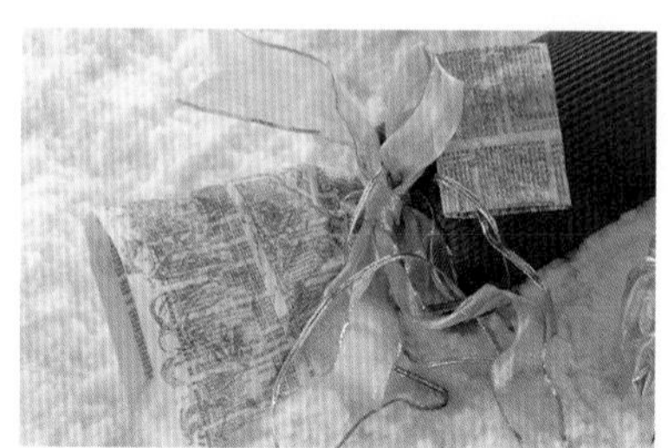

This makes a beautiful and fragrant parcel. Wrap the gift with paper and tie a wide ribbon around it. Tie a tiny bunch of dried lavender and fern with fuse wire, wrap the stems in a narrower, co-ordinating ribbon, and tie to the top of parcel in a bow.

Cracker

This is a great way to disguise a bottle of wine. Decorate two pages of an old telephone directory with a gold glitter pen. Cut a piece of corrugated card to the length of the bottle, and wide enough to wrap around it. Stick one telephone directory page to each of the shorter sides of the card, sticking the right side of the telephone directory to the wrong side of the card, overlapping by about 1cm/½in. Wrap and secure the card tightly around the bottle. Tie the paper ends like cracker ends with gold wired ribbon.

Chocolate crackle

Fill a pretty bowl with home-made chocolates (see page 73) and place in the centre of a large square of cellophane. Bring the corners of the cellophane to a point and tie with a bright ribbon.

Star parcel

Decorate plain paper with potato-printed stars. Cut a potato in half, then using the point of a knife (or a star cutter), score a star shape about 1cm/½in deep. Slice the potato horizontally away from the shape so that the star stands proud. Dip potato into water-based paint and press on to the paper. When dry, wrap round the present and tie with ribbon.

Mr Snowman

Cut a cotton wool pad into a small circle to make the head, use a second larger circle for the body and glue on to the wrapped present. Cut hat, buttons, mouth and eyes from black paper or card, and a nose from red, then glue in position. Attach two pieces of tartan ribbon to make the scarf.

Money bags

Wrap a book in a double layer of green tissue paper and tie with tartan ribbon. Tie a bag of gold chocolate coins on top.

Ivy leaf print

Sponge green acrylic ink on to a large ivy leaf, then randomly stamp the leaf over sheets of tissue paper. Rub the leaf on the wrong side when in position to help define the shape. Finish with big, dramatic bows in ivy green, or in the same colour as your tissue paper.

These lovely sacks will become favourite family heirlooms and the Christmas tree design doubles as a delightful advent calendar – a special present every morning during the month of December will be beyond the wildest imagination of any child. So, make their dreams come true!

christmas *sacks*

Goose sack

YOU WILL NEED

pattern drafting paper • **lightweight iron-on interfacing** • 40cm/16in white felt square • **21cm/8¼in orange felt square** • yellow and black felt scraps for the beak and eye • **2 x 21cm/8¼in green felt squares** • 50 x 150cm/20 x 60in red fabric • **gold crochet thread** • gold puffa paint • **1m of 2cm/¾in gold ribbon** • 2cm/¾in alphabet stencil template • **gold cord**

1 **Make the pattern** Using pattern drafting paper, draw up the pattern pieces from the template on page 122. Cut out goose, wing, legs, beak, eye and holly patterns.

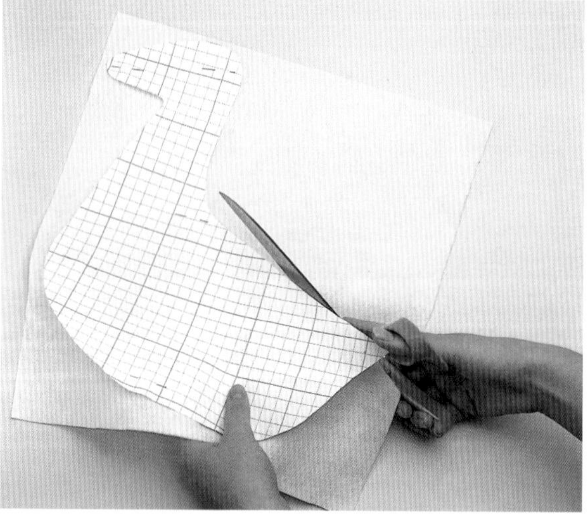

2 **Cut out the felt pieces** Iron the interfacing on to the back of the felt pieces, covering an area just larger than the pattern pieces. Cut out the pattern pieces in the appropriate coloured felt.

3 **Position the felt pieces** Peel off the interfacing backing paper and pin, then iron the felt pieces in place on to one half of the red sack fabric. Allow for 2cm/¾in turnings on the top and side edges.

CHRISTMAS IS COMING AND THE GOOSE IS GETTING FAT

PLEASE PUT A PENNY IN THE OLD MANS HAT

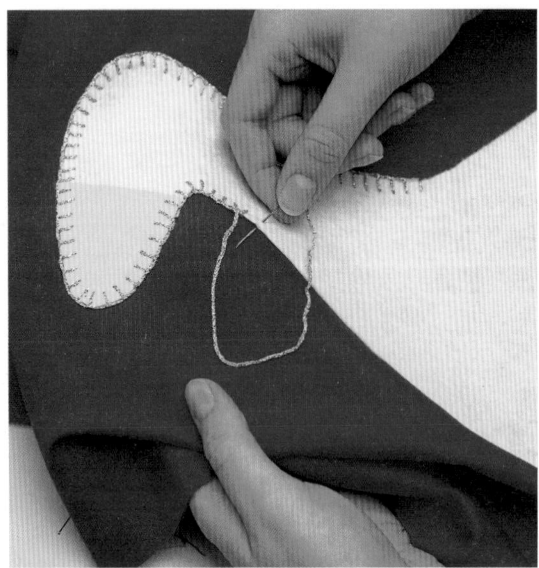

4 Stitch felt pieces in place Use the gold crochet thread to blanket stitch around the felt pieces, to secure. Alternatively, secure with machine zigzag stitch using matching coloured thread. Don't forget the eye and the holly.

6 Pencil in the rhyme Using the stencil, mark out the lettering of the rhyme along the two curved lines. To space them evenly, allow 12 letters and spaces between the four quarters on the top line and 10 on the lower line.

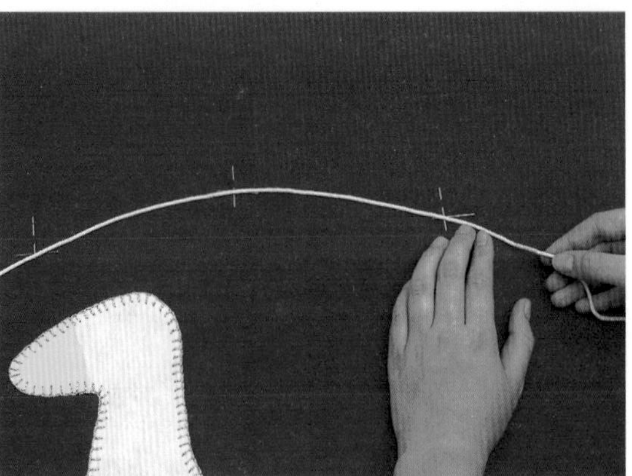

5 Measure out rhyme line Fold the red material in half lengthways to find the centre line, mark A. Fold in half again to find the quarter line, and mark B. Measure and mark with a pin 25cm/10in down from the top corners, 18cm/7in from the top of both lines B, and 15cm/6in from the top of line A.

Mark out rhyme line Following the pin marks, use cord or string to shape the curved line for the lettering. Secure with pins. Turn sack upside down and repeat for the lower line of lettering.

7 Write the rhyme Using the gold puffa paint, write over the pencilled letters.

Add the bow Tie the gold ribbon into a bow, then pin and stitch in place.

Make up the sack With right sides together, pin and stitch the side seams of the sack, then turn under and stitch the top edge to neaten. Remember the seam allowance is 2cm/¾in. Turn right side out and press. Make two hanging loops with the cord, sew to side seams. Finish off top edge with blanket stitch.

Christmas tree sack

YOU WILL NEED

pattern drafting paper • **30 x 90cm/12 x 36in lightweight iron-on interfacing** • 55cm/21½in green felt square • **5cm/2in square brown felt for tree trunk and a larger scrap of orange felt for tub** • 50 x 150cm/20 x 60in red fabric • **matching sewing threads** • 30 x 90cm/12 x 36in gold fabric • **metallic red and silver puffa paints** • 5.5m/6yd of 3mm/⅛in wide red ribbon • **alphabet stencil template (size will depend on length of child's name)** • 1m/1yd gold cord

1 **Make the pattern** Using pattern drafting paper, draw up the pattern pieces from the template on page 123. Carefully cut out the tree, tub and star patterns.

2 **Cut out the felt pieces** Iron the interfacing on to the back of the felt pieces, covering an area just larger than the pattern pieces. Cut out pattern pieces in appropriate coloured felt.
Position the felt pieces Peel off interfacing backing and pin, then iron in place on the red sack fabric. (see step 3 of instructions for Goose sack)

3 **Stitch felt pieces in place** Using matching coloured thread, machine zigzag stitch around the felt tree, trunk and tub to secure them in place.

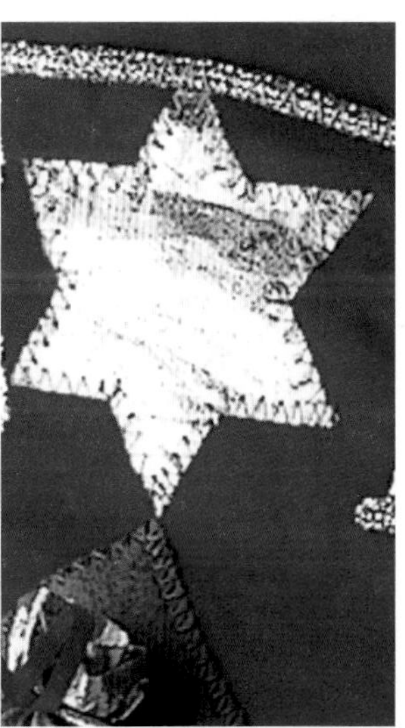

4 **Make gift bags and star** Iron interfacing on to the wrong side of the gold fabric, then mark and cut out 24 rectangles of 6 x 12cm/2½ x 4½in for the gift bags. Cut out one star using the pattern piece. Position the star on the red fabric, at the top of the tree and zigzag stitch in place.

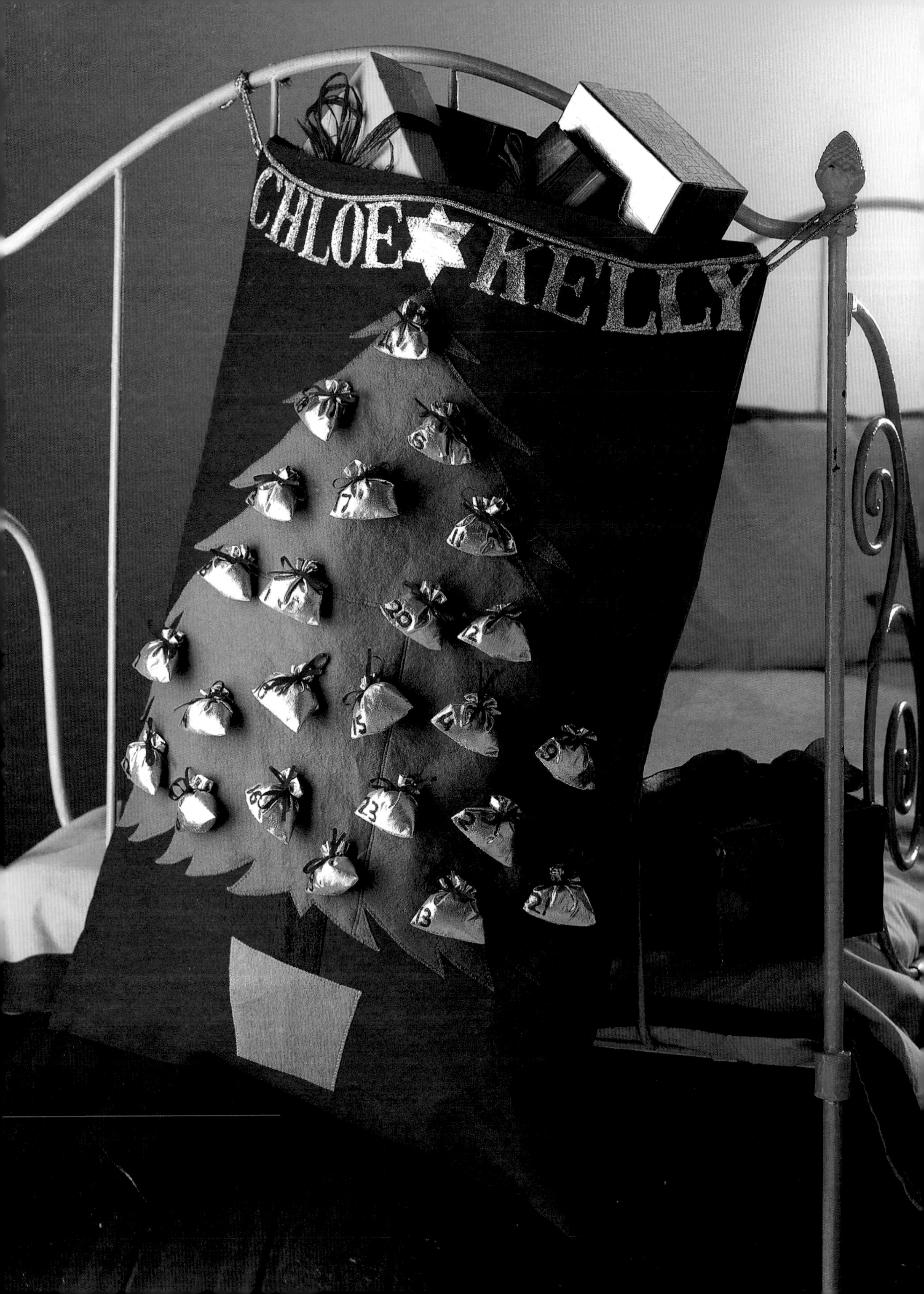
CHLOE
KELLY

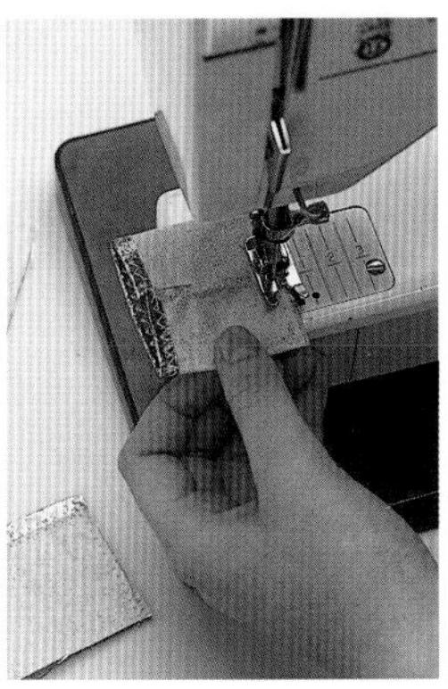

5 Make up each gift bag Turn under 5mm/¼in along one long edge and zigzag stitch in place. Fold fabric in half widthways, with right sides together, and zigzag stitch side seam. Position seam to the centre, then zigzag stitch the lower seam.

6 Number the gift bags Turn the bags right side out and, using red puffa paint, write numbers 1 to 24 in the left-hand corner of each one.

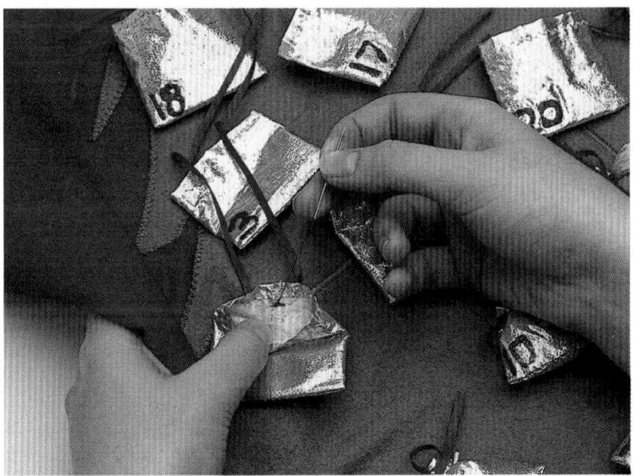

7 Attach the gift bags Cut the ribbon into 24 pieces of 22cm/8½in long. Arrange the bags over the tree and pin in place. Place a ribbon behind each bag and securely hand-stitch each bag and ribbon to the tree.

8 Add the name Using an appropriate sized stencil – it depends on the length of the child's name – pencil in the lettering either side of the star, then fill in each letter with the silver puffa paint.

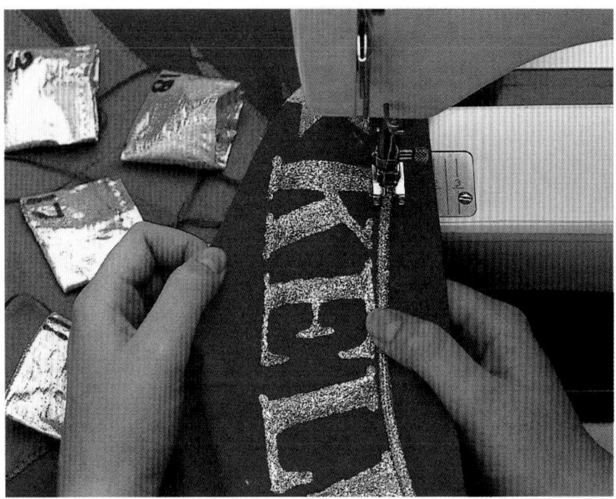

9 Add the cord Pin the gold cord across the top of the lettering from one side of the sack to the other, then zigzag stitch the cord in place. Make two hanging loops with the cord and pin to the side edges near the top.

10 Make up the sack Follow step 7 of instructions for Goose sack, securing the hanging loops in the side seams.

Add the treats Pop a small gift into each bag and close by tying a pretty bow with the ribbon fixed behind the bag.

Hang up the empty sack on 1 December and use as an Advent calendar. When all the gift bags are open, it will be Christmas Eve and the sack will be ready for Father Christmas to fill with goodies.

The joy of edible presents is that they are suitable to give to anyone – and if you've made them yourself they'll be even more appreciated. They look fantastic in pretty jars, boxes or bottles, and wrapped in festive paper and ribbons. These presents are all very simple to make, and can be made well in advance and stored or frozen until needed – remember to stick on an unobtrusive label giving the use-by date and best method of storage.

edible presents

Moroccan preserved lemons

This is a traditional Moroccan condiment. For a spicier result you could add 1 teaspoon coriander seeds, 1 teaspoon black peppercorns and 2 cinnamon sticks to the jar.

10 small lemons
150g/5½oz salt
juice of 6 – 8 large lemons

1 Soak the lemons for 3 days in lukewarm water to soften the skins. Change the water every day.
2 Quarter the lemons lengthways, leaving the stalk end intact. Open up the quarters gently and salt the flesh quite generously. Put a thin layer of salt in a dry, sterilized jar and pack in the lemons and remaining salt and spices, if using.
3 Add the lemon juice to cover the fruit and spices completely. Leave some air space in the top of the jar. Cover, seal and label, then leave to mature in a cool dark place for at least 30 days, shaking daily.
4 The lemons can be removed from the juice as and when required. Rinse of salt before using.

• The lemons will keep in this mixture indefinitely if stored in a dry place.

Cranberry gin

This beautiful ruby-red drink is so festive and makes a stunning looking present – no one will believe it is not shop-bought, especially if you make it in an attractive glass jar such as this one. It is extremely easy to make, and can be prepared well in advance.

Makes about 700ml/1¼ pints

225g/8oz cranberries, washed and dried
1 orange
225g/8oz caster sugar
500ml/18fl oz gin

1 Prick the cranberries all over with a needle. Use a vegetable peeler to remove two long strips of rind from the orange, making sure there is no white pith attached. Put the rind and sugar in a dry, sterilized jar and stir well to release the orange oils.

2 Add the gin, and stir well until the sugar has thoroughly dissolved (it will look a little cloudy). Next, add the cranberries. Cover the jar and leave to mature in a cool dark place for up to 3 months, shaking every few days to extract the full fruit flavour.

Mini gingerbread houses

Makes 4 houses

50g/1¾oz butter
100g/3½oz light muscovado sugar
4 tbsp golden syrup
2 tbsp black treacle
350g/12oz plain flour
1 tbsp ground ginger
1 tbsp bicarbonate of soda
2 eggs, separated
450g/1lb icing sugar, sifted
4 x 15cm/6in thin cakeboards

1 Preheat the oven to 190°C/375°F/Gas 5. Make the templates (see below right) from card. Line two baking sheets with non-stick baking paper. Gently melt the butter, sugar, syrup and treacle.
2 Sift the flour, ginger and bicarbonate of soda into a bowl, then add the egg yolks and the syrup. Mix to a soft dough and knead until smooth.
3 Cut the dough into four pieces and wrap all but one piece in plastic film. Roll out on a lightly floured surface to 3mm/⅛in thick, then using the templates (below right) cut out two roof pieces, two end and two side walls, re-rolling as necessary. Place on the baking sheet. Repeat with remaining dough. Bake for 8–10 minutes until lightly browned. Cool for 5 minutes; transfer to a wire rack.
4 Make the royal icing: stir the egg whites to break up. Add the icing sugar a little at a time, beating well after each addition, until the icing is thick enough to stand up in soft peaks.
5 Pipe beads and loops of icing over the roof pieces. Pipe lines to mark the windows and doors on the side and end walls and infill with beads of icing. Leave to dry in a warm place.
6 Assemble the houses: pipe a line of icing on the side edges of the walls and end pieces. Stick together to form a box shape. Place on a cakeboard. Pipe a line of icing following the roof pitch on the end walls, along the top of the side walls and the top edges of the roof pieces. Press the roof gently in position and leave to set.

Amaretti

These crisp Italian biscuits have a wonderful bitter-sweet flavour.

Makes about 30–34

100g/3½oz whole blanched almonds
50g/1¾oz bitter almonds or dried apricot kernels
150g/5½oz caster sugar
2 tsp Amaretto or a few drops of almond essence
2 egg whites
icing sugar, to dust (optional)

1 Preheat the oven to 180°C/350°F/Gas 4. Line several baking sheets with non-stick baking paper.
2 Place the nuts in a food processor and process until finely ground. Add the sugar, Amaretto and the egg whites and process to a sticky dough.
3 Spoon the mixture into a piping bag with a 1cm/½in nozzle and pipe 2.5cm/1in rounds on the baking sheets. Bake for 15 minutes or until lightly browned. Transfer to a wire rack to cool. Repeat with remaining mixture. Dust with icing sugar, if using.

• Store the amaretti in an airtight tin for 1 month, or freeze for up to 1 month.

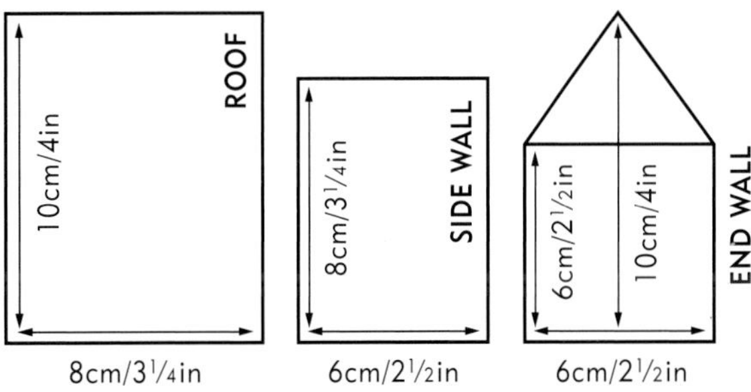

• For the best flavour and texture eat the gingerbread houses within 1 week. They will keep for up to 1 month. Store in cake boxes.

Brown sugar meringues

Dip these melt-in-the-mouth meringues in chocolate and transfer to individual fairy-cake paper cases when giving them as presents. If you want to serve them as a dessert, you can also sandwich them in pairs with cream or chestnut purée.

Makes about 24

100g/3½oz light muscovado sugar
50g/1¾oz caster sugar
3 medium egg whites
½ tsp lemon juice or vinegar

1 Preheat the oven to 150°C/300°F/Gas 2. Put the sugars in a shallow dish and place in the oven, while it heats up, for about 15 minutes, to help remove some of the sugars' stickiness. Line 3 baking sheets with greaseproof paper.
2 Rub all the sugar through a sieve with a wooden spoon to break down any lumps and make it finer. Whisk the egg whites in a large, grease-free bowl until they stand in stiff, dry peaks. Whisk in half the sugar along with the lemon juice or vinegar. Gently fold in the remaining sugar with a large metal spoon.
3 Shape the meringues into ovals using 2 teaspoons and arrange them on the greaseproof paper. Put into the oven and reduce the temperature to 110°C/225°F/Gas ¼. Cook for 1½–2 hours until firm and dry. Turn the oven off but leave the meringues inside until they are cold.

• Store in an airtight container for up to 3 weeks, or freeze for 6 months.

Mixed nut praline

This caramelized nut mixture makes great grown-up nut brittle. Like the Brown sugar meringues, transfer the sweets to small fairy-cake paper cases. They will delight the 'sweet-tooths' in your family. You can also crush the brittle into crumbs to decorate cakes and desserts or even powder it in a coffee grinder to add to meringue or buttercream.

Makes about 20 sweets

175g/6oz unblanched shelled mixed whole nuts (eg hazelnuts, peanuts, almonds), toasted
250g/9oz caster sugar

1 Lightly oil a heavy baking sheet. Chop the nuts roughly. Put into a large heavy-based saucepan

with the sugar and stir over a low heat until the sugar has melted.

2 Stop stirring, but continue cooking until the sugar is golden and caramelized – don't allow it to become too dark or it will taste bitter. Quickly pour the praline on to the baking sheet. Spread it out and leave it to set hard.

3 Shatter the praline into pieces and transfer to the fairy-cake cases.

• The praline can be stored in a jar or tin for up to 2 months.

Gingerbread window biscuits

Makes 20

half quantity Gingerbread dough (see Mini gingerbread houses recipe, page 69)
250g/9oz coloured clear sweets
3mm/⅛in wide coloured ribbons (optional)

1 Preheat the oven to 190°C/375°F/Gas 5. Make the gingerbread dough to the end of step 2 of the Mini gingerbread houses recipe. Roll out on a lightly floured surface to 3mm/⅛in thick.

2 Using *vol-au-vent* cutters, cut out the shapes removing the centre pieces. Or, use festive cutters and cut out the centres using smaller cutters or a sharp knife, cutting out the pattern freehand.

3 Transfer to the baking sheets and place a sweet in the centre of each biscuit. Using a drinking straw, make a hole in the tops, if you want to be able to hang them up. Bake for 8–10 minutes or until the sweets have melted and the dough is golden brown.

4 Cool on the baking sheets, then thread ribbons through, if you are using the biscuits as decorations.

• For the best flavour and texture eat within 1 week. The biscuits will keep for up to 1 month. Store in cake boxes.

Lebkuchen

These traditional biscuits, made for hundreds of years in Austria and Germany, have a lovely texture, somewhere between a cake and a biscuit. The combination of ginger and cinnamon makes them taste especially Christmassy.

Makes about 36

FOR THE BISCUITS

50g/1¾oz butter
225g/8oz clear honey
2 tbsp milk
225g/8oz plain flour
1 tsp bicarbonate of soda
1 tbsp cocoa powder
2 tbsp cornflour
1 tsp cinnamon
1 tsp ginger

FOR THE DECORATION

1 tbsp icing sugar
1 tbsp caster sugar
½ tsp cornflour
25g/1oz butter, melted
100g/3½oz plain chocolate

1 Put the butter, honey and milk in a pan and bring slowly to the boil. In a large bowl, sift the remaining biscuit ingredients together. Remove the pan from the heat, add to the sifted mixture and stir until smooth. Cover with plastic film and leave until cool enough to handle.

2 Preheat the oven to 180°C/350°F/Gas 4. Line 2 baking trays with greaseproof paper. Knead the biscuit mixture gently until smooth. Roll out on a lightly floured surface to 1cm/½in thickness. Stamp out shapes with 5cm/2in cutters. Arrange on the trays and bake for 10–12 minutes until risen.

3 Meanwhile, for the decoration, sift together the sugars and cornflour. Remove the biscuits from the oven. Put half on a rack and brush the tops with the melted butter. Sift the sugar-mix over and leave to set. Allow all the biscuits to cool.

4 Melt the chocolate in a bowl over a pan of simmering water. Set the rack with the plain biscuits over a tray. Spoon the chocolate over them, coating the tops and sides. Leave to set.

- Store in an airtight tin for up to 6 days.
- To make ahead: open-freeze the sugar-coated biscuits and pack in a freezer bag. Freeze the others without their chocolate coating for up to 2 months. Thaw the biscuits for 2 hours at room temperature, then coat the plain biscuits with chocolate, following step 4 above.

Luxury dark chocolate and Grand Marnier truffles

This selection of fresh cream truffles, each flavoured with a different liqueur, makes an irresistible Christmas gift for the chocaholics among your family and friends.

Makes 25–30 truffles

225g/8oz dark chocolate, broken into pieces
150ml/¼ pint double cream
2 tbsp Grand Marnier or Cointreau
grated rind of 1 orange
cocoa powder, for coating

1 Melt the chocolate in a bowl over gently simmering water, stir in the cream, liqueur and orange rind.
2 Chill for 1 hour, or until firm, then roll teaspoons of the mixture into balls before rolling in cocoa powder.

Milk chocolate and coffee liqueur truffles

Make as opposite but with milk chocolate, and replace the orange rind with two teaspoons of instant coffee granules. Flavour with Tia Maria and coat in coarsely grated milk chocolate.

White chocolate and Amaretto truffles

Make as opposite but with white chocolate, and replace the orange rind and Grand Marnier with Amaretto. Coat in finely grated white chocolate.

- To freeze: pack into a rigid container before rolling in cocoa or grated chocolate, interleaving the layers with freezer film. Use within two months.
- From the freezer: thaw in the fridge, then roll in cocoa powder or grated milk or white chocolate.

CHAPTER THREE

festive entertaining

This is the season to be jolly, and there will be plenty of time over Christmas to gather friends and family round you for festive celebrations.

I'm not going to give you an hour-by-hour, minute-by-minute countdown to the big day, but rather some ideas and inspirations for informal yet elegant get-togethers that won't involve you slaving in the kitchen for hours – leaving you free to welcome your guests for a relaxed evening.

This Christmas Eve supper holds all the promise of the festivities to come. The easy menu is simple yet elegant. It not only looks good but remains delicious for hours, so it's perfect for any late arrivals. Prepare in advance to give yourself plenty of time to join in the fun.

christmas eve supper

Smoked fish pâté with walnuts and grapes

This can be made the day before. Serve spooned on to plates or in individual pots.

Serves 8

900g/2lb smoked cod
2 tbsp milk
200g/7oz light cream cheese
3 tbsp creamed horseradish
freshly ground black pepper
paprika, for sprinkling
mixed salad leaves and fresh herbs (optional)
140g/5oz seedless green and seedless red grapes
50g/2oz broken walnuts
2 lemons
4 tbsp walnut or olive oil

1 Simmer the fish in a covered pan with the milk for 5 minutes, or until just cooked through. Drain thoroughly and leave to cool, then roughly flake.
2 Beat the cream cheese in a bowl with the horseradish, then stir in the flaked fish and season to taste with black pepper. Stir gently to combine. Spoon into a serving dish or individual pots, cover and chill until ready to serve.
3 Spoon the pâté on to plates, or leave in the pots and sprinkle with paprika. Garnish with salad leaves and herbs, the grapes and walnuts. Pare the rind from the lemons and scatter over the pâté. Mix one tablespoon of lemon juice with the oil and spoon over the salad.

Lamb couscous with tomato harissa

Make this spicy lamb dish a day in advance, then simply add the chickpeas, raisins and aubergines when reheating. Harissa is fiery North African chilli sauce. Serve the tomato harissa in a jug for those who want an extra 'hot' flavour.

Serves 8

2 medium aubergines, thinly sliced
8 tbsp olive oil
900g/2lb diced leg of lamb
2 onions, sliced
3 celery sticks, thinly sliced
25g/1oz fresh root ginger, grated
4 garlic cloves, sliced
1 tbsp ground turmeric
1/2 tsp chilli powder
2 cinnamon sticks, broken in half
good pinch saffron strands
400g can chopped tomatoes
600ml/1 pint lamb or chicken stock
2 x 400g cans chickpeas, drained
25g/1oz raisins
2 tsp harissa paste, or hot chilli sauce
salt and freshly ground black pepper

FOR THE COUSCOUS

finely grated rind of 2 lemons, plus 1 tbsp fresh lemon juice
55g/2oz butter, melted
8 tbsp roughly chopped fresh coriander
500g/1lb 2oz couscous
700ml/1 1/4 pints boiling water

1 Brush the aubergine slices with a little oil and lightly fry on both sides. Reserve.
2 Heat the remaining oil in a large frying pan, add the lamb in batches and fry quickly to brown, then remove from the pan with a slotted spoon. Add the onions and celery and fry for 5 minutes, then return the lamb to the pan with the ginger, garlic and spices.
3 Add half the can of tomatoes to the pan with the stock and bring to the boil. Cover and simmer very gently for 1 hour or until the lamb is tender. Stir in the chickpeas, raisins and aubergines, then continue to simmer for another 20 minutes.
4 Drain four tablespoons of stock from the pan and blend in a food processor with the reserved tomatoes, harissa paste and season to taste. Transfer to a small jug.
5 For the couscous: mix together the lemon rind and juice, butter, coriander and seasoning. Place the couscous in a large, shallow ovenproof serving dish and pour over the boiling water. Cover with foil and leave for 5 minutes. Add the coriander mixture, fluff up with a fork and serve with the lamb.

French bean and tomato salad

This dish can be served warm or cold.

Serves 8

450g/1lb small tomatoes, halved
1 tsp caster sugar
675g/1½ lb French beans
½ small red onion, grated
6 tbsp extra virgin olive oil
salt and freshly ground black pepper
roughly chopped flatleaf parsley, to garnish

1 Preheat the grill to hot. Place the tomatoes in a shallow heatproof dish, cut sides up, then sprinkle with sugar and season. Grill for 3 minutes or until slightly softened, then leave to cool.

2 Cook the beans in boiling, salted water for 2 minutes or until just tender. Drain and mix in a bowl with the tomatoes, onion, oil and seasoning. Serve sprinkled with parsley.

Oatmeal flummery with whisky oranges

Make both the flummery and oranges a day in advance, then chill until ready to serve.

Serves 8

6 oranges, plus 4 tbsp fresh orange juice
8 kumquats, thinly sliced
15g/½ oz light muscovado sugar
6 tbsp whisky
50g/2oz medium oatmeal
250ml/9fl oz quark
6 tbsp clear honey
300ml/½ pint double cream, lightly whisked

1 Finely grate the rind from two oranges and reserve. Cut the skins away from all the oranges, and thinly slice the fruit. Place in a bowl with the kumquats, the sugar and half the whisky. Toss lightly, cover and chill for at least 1 hour.
2 Place the oatmeal in a dry frying pan and lightly toast for 2 minutes over a medium heat, then leave to cool.
3 Whisk together the quark, honey, grated orange rind and juice and the remaining whisky, then fold in the cream and oatmeal.
4 Spoon into serving glasses and chill. Decorate the flummery with orange and kumquat slices and serve the remaining fruit separately.

There's nothing like a glass of something warm and spicy on cold winter nights and the smell and taste of a mulled drink always reminds me of Christmas. Here are some traditional ideas for mulled drinks, from a classic mulled red wine, to the lesser known, but equally delicious mulled cider and ale.

mulled drinks

Classic mulled red wine

For each bottle of red wine used, add 150ml/¼ pint ruby port (this can be basic quality), and about 75ml/2½ fl oz each of cognac and either Cointreau or Grand Marnier. Add one or two tablespoons of light muscovado sugar, depending on how sweet you want the mull to be. Add a couple of cinnamon sticks, a whole nutmeg, a couple of bay leaves and as many clove-studded orange and lemon slices as there are guests. Stir initially to dissolve the sugar, then heat gently until piping hot – do not allow to boil.

Gluhwein

The cup that cheers on the Alpine pistes is also drunk at Christmas in Germany and Austria. For each bottle of red wine, add 125ml/4fl oz cognac or German brandy (such as Asbach), 50ml/2fl oz golden or dark rum, two cinnamon sticks, two tablespoons of light muscovado sugar, and clove-studded lemon slices. Stir to dissolve the sugar, then heat gently until piping hot – do not boil.

Hot cider punch

For each 1 litre/1¾ pints bottle of cider used, add 125ml/4fl oz each of rum and either calvados or English apple brandy, three cinnamon sticks, one tablespoon of light muscovado sugar, and some clove-studded cored apple slices. Stir, then heat gently until piping hot – do not allow to boil.

Mulled ale

For each 1 litre/1¾ pints of beer (Scottish golden ale is particularly good), add 100ml/3½ fl oz each of cognac and medium-dry sherry, 150ml/¼ pint water, two tablespoons of light muscovado sugar, two teaspoons each of nutmeg and ground ginger, two cinnamon sticks and several clove-studded lemon slices. Stir, then heat gently until piping hot – do not allow to boil.

Tea punch

Into a heated punchbowl, pour 150ml/¼ pint each of cognac and the darkest rum you can find, plus the juice of one lemon. Stir in two tablespoons of light muscovado sugar, then pour on about 1 litre/1¾ pints of hot, freshly made, strong black tea. Add more sugar to taste, and float lemon slices on top.

The festive season is a great time to catch up with family and friends, a tasty nibble in one hand and a glass of something special in the other, but it can be very stressful for the cook, as traditional party food is often fiddly to prepare. So why not try these stylish suggestions for a drinks party for twenty guests, which can be made and served within two hours, If you make use of the freezer, the preparation can be broken down into convenient moments during the Christmas run-up.

christmas drinks party

Vegetable crisps

Makes about 1kg/2lb

3 medium raw beetroot
2 sweet potatoes
oil, for deep frying
sea salt

1 Peel the beetroot and sweet potatoes, then slice thinly, either by hand or using the slicing blade of a food processor. Sprinkle with salt and dry well on kitchen paper.
2 Heat the oil to 180°C/350°F or until a slice of vegetable added to it rises to the surface instantly and starts to brown. Add vegetable slices in batches and fry until crisp and golden. Serve piled up on a plate and sprinkled with sea salt.

Pesto and red pepper omelette

Cook this the day before, then store in the fridge. Bring back to room temperature before serving.

Serves 20

400g jar pimentos in salted water, drained and finely chopped
3 tbsp green pesto
8 eggs, beaten
2 tbsp olive oil
seasoning

1 Mix together the pimentos, pesto and eggs, then season well. Heat the oil in a large frying pan, preferably non-stick, pour in the egg mixture and cover with a lid or foil. Cook gently for about 12–15 minutes until the egg is almost set. Place a plate over the omelette, then turn the pan over to transfer it to the plate. Slide the omelette back into the pan and continue cooking for a further 3–5 minutes until the mixture is set. Slide on to a plate and leave until cold.

2 Wrap in foil and chill until ready to serve, then cut into squares or diamonds and arrange on a plate.

Cherry tomato, tapenade and goat's cheese puffs

Makes 32

375g packet ready-rolled puff pastry, thawed if frozen
3 tbsp tapenade (black olive paste)
350g/12oz cherry tomatoes, sliced
100g/4oz firm goat's cheese, chopped
seasoning

1 Preheat the oven to 220°C/425°F/Gas 7. Unroll the pastry and cut into eight pieces crossways and four lengthways. Arrange the squares, a little apart, on two dampened baking sheets. Spread a little of the tapenade on each square. Place a few of the tomato slices on top, followed by a little goat's cheese. Sprinkle with salt and plenty of freshly ground black pepper, then bake for 12–15 minutes until puffed up and golden. Serve warm or cold.

Jasmine rice with prawns wrapped in spinach

Makes 40

225g/8oz Thai jasmine rice
225g/8oz cooked peeled prawns
2.5cm/1in piece fresh root ginger, finely chopped
4 spring onions, finely chopped
2 tsp light soy sauce
225g/8oz large spinach leaves
seasoning
banana or large cabbage leaves, to serve

1 Place the rice in a pan with 450ml/¾ pint water and a little salt. Bring to the boil, then cover and cook for 10 minutes. Remove the pan from the heat and leave to stand, covered, for 5 minutes. Remove the lid and leave the rice to go cold.
2 Chop the prawns and mix together with the ginger, spring onions and soy sauce, then stir into the cooked rice. Remove any thick spines from the spinach leaves, then blanch the leaves for a few seconds in a large pan of boiling water until they have just turned bright green. Drain immediately and cool quickly under cold running water. Pat leaves dry with kitchen paper.
3 Spread four sheets of plastic film over the work surface. Arrange the spinach leaves on each piece of plastic film to form 15 x 25cm/6 x 10in rectangles, overlapping the leaves to ensure there are no gaps.
4 Spread the rice mixture thinly over the leaves, pressing it down with moistened hands. Roll up the spinach leaves tightly from the long edges to enclose the filling. Wrap each roll tightly in plastic film; chill for at least an hour.
5 To serve, slice each roll into 10 pieces; arrange on a platter lined with banana or cabbage leaves.

Turkey and bacon bites

All the flavour of Christmas rolled into a single delicious bite.

Makes 32

4 x 100g/4oz turkey fillets
25g/1oz butter
1 shallot, finely chopped
½ tsp dried thyme
1 tbsp chopped fresh parsley
1 tsp finely grated lemon rind
75g/3oz fresh white breadcrumbs
1 egg, beaten
50g/2oz cranberries, thawed if frozen
225g/8oz rindless streaky bacon, thinly sliced
seasoning
bay leaves, to garnish

1 Preheat the oven to 200°C/400°F/Gas 6. Sandwich each of the turkey fillets between two large sheets of plastic film and flatten with a rolling pin.
2 Heat the butter in a pan, add the shallot and fry gently for 5 minutes until softened. Remove from the heat, stir in the thyme, parsley, lemon rind, breadcrumbs, egg and seasoning and mix well.
3 Spread the stuffing over the turkey fillets and press down lightly. Arrange the cranberries along the length of the stuffing. Roll up each turkey fillet from one long edge. Wrap the bacon slices, overlapping slightly, end to end around the turkey rolls.
4 Transfer the rolls to a metal baking dish and roast for 20–25 minutes until the bacon is crisp and the turkey tender. Remove and spear at 2.5cm/1in intervals with eight cocktail sticks, then slice between the sticks. Serve warm or cold on bay leaves.

• To freeze, cook and cool quickly, then wrap in foil and freeze for up to 1 month. Defrost in fridge, then either serve cold or heat well at 180°C/350°F/Gas 4 for 15 minutes. Slice and serve.

Left: *Corn and salami muffins (recipe opposite above)*

Corn and salami muffins

Serve these muffins piled into the centre of a scooped-out green cabbage.

Makes 40

100g/4oz self-raising flour
75g/3oz corn or maize meal
1 tsp baking powder
1 tsp dried mustard
½ tsp salt
50g/2oz pepper salami, finely chopped
50g/2oz mature Cheddar, finely cubed
40g/1½ oz Parmesan, finely grated
50g/2oz butter, melted and cooled slightly
150ml/¼ pint milk
1 egg, beaten

1 Preheat the oven to 200°C/400°F/Gas 6. Grease two large baking sheets. Mix together the flour, corn or maize meal, baking powder, dried mustard and salt. Stir in the salami, the Cheddar and 25g/1oz of the Parmesan.
2 Stir in the butter, milk and egg and mix to a soft consistency. Leave to stand for 5 minutes, then drop teaspoons of the mixture, a little apart, on to the baking sheets. Sprinkle the reserved Parmesan over the top, then bake for 15–20 minutes until risen and golden brown. Serve warm.

• To freeze, allow the muffins to go cold, then pack them into freezer bags. Before serving, defrost, then reheat in a hot oven for 5 minutes.

Spiced lamb and sesame nuggets

A thick slice of red cabbage makes a perfect base for these. I would not recommend cooking these ahead of serving, as reheating may dry them out. Prepare and shape, then keep chilled for up to 12 hours until ready to cook.

Makes 40

25g/1oz fresh coriander
1 large onion, chopped
1kg/2lb minced lamb
50g/2oz toasted breadcrumbs
4 tsp curry paste, preferably red Thai
2 tbsp fresh lemon juice
2 tbsp sesame seeds
1 tbsp sunflower oil
seasoning

1 Process the coriander and onion in a food processor until very finely chopped. Add the lamb, breadcrumbs, curry paste, lemon juice and seasoning; mix well.
2 Shape the mixture into about 40 teaspoon-sized balls and sprinkle with the sesame seeds, then chill until ready to cook. Heat the oil in a large pan, such as a paella pan, then add the nuggets and fry quickly on all sides for about 10 minutes until evenly browned. Serve warm, speared on cocktail sticks.

Prosciutto and mozzarella squares

Makes 50

350g/12oz strong white bread flour
1 tsp salt
2 tsp dried mixed herbs
1½ tsp easy-blend dried yeast
200ml/7fl oz hand-hot water
1 tbsp olive oil
2 tbsp sun-dried tomato paste
50g/2oz prosciutto, thinly sliced
150g/5oz mozzarella, very thinly sliced
beaten egg, to glaze
sea salt

1 Mix together the flour, salt, herbs and yeast in a bowl. Add the water and oil and mix to a soft dough. Turn out on to a lightly floured surface and knead for about 5 minutes until it is smooth and no longer sticky.

2 Roll out half the dough thinly to line a 23 x 33/9 x 13in oiled Swiss roll tin. Spread the tomato paste on top and cover with the prosciutto, then the mozzarella. Roll out the remaining dough and use to cover filling. Leave to stand in a warm place for 15 minutes.

3 Preheat the oven to 220°C/425°F/Gas 7. Brush the top of the dough with the egg, then sprinkle with sea salt. Leave to rise for 15 minutes, then bake for 20–25 minutes until the top is crisp and golden brown. Leave to cool in the tin for 5 minutes, then cut into 50 rectangles. Serve warm.

• To freeze, make up recipe to the end of step 2, then cover with freezer foil and freeze. To serve, defrost thoroughly at room temperature, then bake as above.

Stilton and apple dip

This dip looks great served in scooped-out green eating apples.

Makes about 450ml/¾ pint

100g/4oz Stilton, crumbled
2 tbsp ready-made apple sauce
1 tbsp fresh lemon juice
1 tsp Dijon mustard
1 tsp clear honey
225g/8oz low-fat yogurt
seasoning
scooped-out green eating apples and celery sticks, to serve

1 Mix together all the ingredients, then spoon into the hollowed-out apples or a bowl; serve with the celery sticks, which you can also serve in a hollowed-out apple.

Smoked salmon dip

To serve the dip in scooped-out lemons, cut a thin slice off the base of each lemon to stabilize it.

Makes about 450ml/¾ pint

100g/4oz smoked salmon trimmings, roughly chopped
80g packet soft cheese with garlic and herbs
2 tsp horseradish sauce
dash of Tabasco sauce
175g/6oz low fat bio yogurt
seasoning
scooped-out fresh lemons and cucumber sticks, to serve

1 Place the smoked salmon trimmings and cheese in a food processor or blender and process until finely chopped. Add all the remaining ingredients and process briefly. Spoon into scooped-out lemons or a bowl and serve with the cucumber sticks.

Here is the perfect menu for feeding a crowd on New Year's Eve. The recipes are easy to make and not too hard on the pocket. Many of them can be made in advance, and several can also be frozen. The food looks fantastic and tastes just great, with lots of textures and colours – and, above all, flavours you'll love.

new year's eve supper

Left to right: *Salmon wreath; Lemon and chilli chicken with Thai dipping sauce; Mozzarella and tomato doughnuts; Butter bean and carrot salad with coconut dressing; Winter vegetable salad with mustard dressing; Leek and Gruyère tart; Marinated mushroom and parsley salad.*

Salmon wreath

This pie is quick to make and can be cooked on the morning of the party. It can also be frozen unbaked for a month.

Serves 12

300g/10½ oz full fat soft cheese
75g/3oz watercress
rind of 1 lemon, plus juice of ½ lemon
2 garlic cloves, crushed
2 x 250g packs puff pastry
600g/1lb 5oz salmon fillet, skinned
1 egg, beaten
freshly ground black pepper

1 Preheat oven to 220°C/425°F/Gas 7. Put the soft cheese, watercress, lemon rind and juice, garlic and pepper in a food processor or blender and whizz until smooth.
2 Roll out each piece of puff pastry to a rectangle about 38 x 18cm/15 x 7in. Cut 2.5cm/1in strip from the long sides of each and set aside for decoration. Overlap two short ends of the rectangles slightly to make one long strip. Dampen the join with water and secure.
3 Cut the salmon into long strips. Arrange evenly in the centre, along the length of the pastry. Spread the cheese mixture over the salmon. Dampen one long pastry edge with water, then bring the other side of the pastry up over the filling and secure the edges. Roll over so the join is underneath. Arrange in a ring on a baking sheet, overlapping the ends slightly; dampen to secure.
4 Using the leftover pastry, cut a long thin strip and shape into a bow at the top of the wreath; secure with beaten egg. Cut out holly leaves and berries; decorate the wreath, securing each leaf and berry in place. Brush wreath with beaten egg. Bake for 30 minutes until brown.

• Freeze, unbaked, wrapped in foil, for up to 1 month.

Lemon and chilli chicken with Thai dipping sauce

The chicken and the dip can be made a day in advance – cool the chicken completely, wrap tightly in foil and chill. Pour dip into a rigid container and chill.

Serves 12

6 boneless skinless chicken breasts, about 150g/5oz each
2 tsp finely grated lemon rind
1 tbsp sunflower oil
½ tsp chilli powder
200ml/7fl oz white wine vinegar
100g/4oz caster sugar
1 red chilli, seeded and finely chopped
salt and pepper
1 cucumber, to serve

1 Preheat oven to 190°C/375°F/Gas 5. Place chicken in a roasting tin. Combine the lemon rind, oil, chilli powder and salt and pepper. Spread over the chicken. Roast for 25–30 minutes until golden. Leave to cool; chill until ready to serve.
2 Make the dip: gently heat the vinegar and sugar in a pan, stirring until the sugar has dissolved. Boil hard for 2–3 minutes until the mixture forms a light syrup. Pour into a serving bowl and stir in the chopped chilli; leave to cool.
3 Slice the cucumber in long diagonal slices, then cut each slice in half. Cut the chicken into thick slices lengthways. Place the bowl of dip in the centre of a platter and surround with the chicken and cucumber slices.

Mozzarella and tomato doughnuts

Makes 24

For the dough

225g/8oz strong white bread flour
½ tsp salt
freshly ground black pepper
2 tsp easy-blend dried yeast
25g/1oz grated Parmesan, plus extra for sprinkling
1 tbsp olive oil
100ml/3½fl oz hand-hot water
1 small egg, beaten

For the Filling

4 pieces of sun-dried tomato
75g/3oz mozzarella
vegetable oil, for deep frying

1 Make the dough: mix the flour, salt, pepper, yeast and Parmesan in a bowl. Mix the oil and water together, then add to the flour with the egg and mix to a soft dough. Turn out on to a lightly

floured surface and knead for about 5 minutes until the dough is smooth and no longer sticky.
2 Cut each piece of tomato into six. Cut the mozzarella into 24 chunks. Divide the dough into 24 equal pieces, then press out to flatten and place a piece of tomato and mozzarella in the centre. Draw up the dough over the filling, pinching it to enclose. Place the doughnuts on a greased baking sheet, set a little apart.
3 Cover the doughnuts with oiled polythene and leave to rise for about 1 hour until the dough springs back when pressed.
4 Heat the oil to 180°C/350°F in a deep pan, or until a cube of bread rises to the surface and is golden. Fry the doughnuts, a few at a time, for about 5 minutes until golden brown. Drain on kitchen paper and serve sprinkled with Parmesan.

• Freeze for up to 1 month. To serve, defrost then warm in the oven or deep fry for 1 minute.

Leek and Gruyère tart

Replacing the ham with sun-dried tomatoes makes a perfect treat for vegetarians. *(Illustrated on page 93.)*

Serves 6

1 tbsp olive oil
450g/1lb leeks, sliced
1/2 tsp dried thyme
1 tsp granulated sugar
2 thick slices smoked ham
100g/4oz cherry tomatoes, halved
40g/1 1/2oz Gruyère, grated

For the pastry

175g/6oz self-raising flour
50g/2oz butter
75g/3oz Gruyère, grated
1/4 tsp cayenne powder
6-8 tbsp milk, to mix

1 Preheat the oven to 200°C/400°F/Gas 6. Heat the oil in a frying pan and fry the leeks until softened. Stir in the thyme and sugar; cook for about 5 minutes until the leeks start to brown.
2 Make the pastry: put the flour in a bowl, add the butter and rub in with your fingertips until the mixture resembles fine breadcrumbs. Stir in the Gruyère and the cayenne, then add the milk and mix to a soft dough. Knead briefly, then place in the centre of a baking sheet. Roll out to a 23cm/9in round.
3 Using a slotted spoon, transfer the leeks to the top of the pastry, almost to the edge. Cut the ham into thin strips and arrange in a cartwheel over the top. Pile the tomatoes in the centre; sprinkle with the Gruyère. Bake for about 25-30 minutes until the pastry is golden brown. Cut into wedges to serve.

• Open freeze, unbaked, until firm, then wrap in foil and freeze for up to 1 month. Defrost on a baking sheet and bake as described above.

Butter bean and carrot salad with coconut dressing

This salad can be made 2–3 days ahead. Mix all the ingredients, apart from the coriander, in a bowl, cover and chill. Add the coriander just before serving.

Serves 12

2 x 400g cans butter beans, drained
450g/1lb carrots, peeled and grated
1 bunch fresh coriander, roughly chopped

FOR THE DRESSING

200ml carton coconut cream
2 tsp red Thai curry paste
3 tbsp sunflower oil
1 tbsp fresh lemon or lime juice
salt and pepper

Mix together the butter beans, carrots and coriander. Blend the dressing ingredients together, then add to the salad, mixing well.

Winter vegetable salad with mustard dressing

Once you've hollowed out the pumpkin, use the flesh for a tasty mash. Chop, cook and mash with butter and salt and pepper.

Serves 12

1 kg/2lb 4oz waxy potatoes
4 celery sticks, sliced diagonally
450g/1lb broccoli, cut into small florets
hollowed-out pumpkin, to serve

FOR THE DRESSING

2 tbsp wholegrain mustard
2 tbsp fresh lemon juice
1 tsp paprika
200ml carton crème fraîche
salt and pepper

1 Cook the potatoes until just tender, then cut into cubes when cool enough to handle. Blanch the celery and broccoli for 3–4 minutes, then drain and refresh under running cold water.
2 Blend the dressing ingredients in a bowl, then pour over the vegetables. Mix well and serve piled into a hollowed-out pumpkin.

Marinated mushroom and parsley salad

It's essential you marinate the mushrooms for at least 1 hour, but you can also do this up to 6 hours in advance.

450g/1lb mixed mushrooms, such as chestnut, oyster and button
1 small red onion, thinly sliced
grated rind of ½ lemon, plus juice of 1 lemon
1 garlic clove, chopped
1 tsp clear honey
7 tbsp olive oil
salt and pepper
25g/1oz chopped fresh parsley
radicchio leaves, to serve

1 Wipe the mushrooms and slice into a bowl. Place the sliced onion in a separate bowl with the lemon rind, juice, garlic and honey. Leave for 5 minutes to soften the onion, then stir in the oil, salt and pepper.
2 Pour the dressing over the mushrooms, mixing well. Leave for at least an hour to allow the marinade to flavour the mushrooms. Just before serving, stir in the parsley and spoon on to radicchio leaves.

Orange and raspberry trifle

It's worth making the custard yourself for this dessert, but if time is short you can use a ready-made one instead. *(Illustrated on page 99.)*

Serves 12

3 oranges
4 cardamom pods
450ml/¾ pint milk
4 egg yolks
150g/5oz caster sugar
2 tbsp sherry
100g/4oz amaretti biscuits, roughly crushed
225g/8oz raspberries, fresh or frozen
1 bought Madeira cake, sliced
500ml carton crème fraîche

1 Peel the rind from the two oranges, taking care not to include any pith. Place four strips of rind (reserve the rest) in a pan with the cardamom pods and milk and gently bring to the boil. Remove from the heat and leave to infuse; remove the pods. In a bowl over a pan of hot water, whisk together the egg yolks and 50g/2oz sugar until light, thick and fluffy (about 5 minutes). Whisk in the hot milk, then return to the pan and cook over a gentle heat until thickened; do not allow to boil. Pour into a bowl and cool.
2 Squeeze the juice from the oranges and mix with the sherry. Place the biscuits and raspberries in a trifle bowl and arrange the cake slices on top. Sprinkle over the orange and sherry mixture.
3 When cool, pour the custard over the trifle. Cut the reserved peel into matchsticks. Place in a pan with the remaining sugar and 100ml/3½fl oz water; bring to the boil. Cook gently for 10 minutes until the orange rind is softened, then boil hard to form a thick syrup that coats the strips. Remove the strips from the syrup with a fork and place on a plate to dry.
4 Just before serving, spoon the crème fraîche over the custard and sprinkle with the orange strips.

Croquembouche

This spectacular cone of choux buns is well worth the effort. It must be finished on the day, and you'll need someone to hold the cone for you while you fill it with the caramel-coated buns.

Serves 20

280g/10oz plain flour
225g/8oz butter
8 eggs
1kg/2lb 4oz caster sugar
gold and silver dragées or almonds, to decorate

FOR THE CONE

cardboard
foil
sticky tape
stapler
oil, for greasing

1 Preheat the oven to 200°C/400°F/Gas 6. Make the cone: cut a semi-circle with a 50cm/20in radius from the cardboard. Cover one side with foil; secure with sticky tape. Roll the cardboard into a cone shape (with the foil inside), so the base measures about 30cm/12in diameter. Secure with sticky tape and staples. Grease the inside with oil. Lightly oil three large baking sheets.

2 Sift the flour on to a plate. Place the butter and 600ml/1 pint water in a large pan; bring slowly to the boil. When the liquid is boiling and the butter has melted, remove from the heat and immediately tip in all the flour in one go. Beat until you have a soft ball that comes away from the sides of the pan.

3 Cool for about 5 minutes, then gradually beat in the eggs to form a soft, shiny mixture. Dot half teaspoonfuls of the mixture over the baking sheets, spaced well apart. You should have about 100 choux buns. Bake for 20–25 minutes until puffed and golden; remove from the oven and prick each bun with a skewer. Return to the oven for 5 minutes; cool on a wire rack.

4 Place the sugar in a large pan with 8 tablespoons of water. Bring to the boil slowly, stirring until the sugar has dissolved. If the sugar starts to crystallize on the sides, brush the crystals down with a damp pastry brush. Cook, without stirring, until the sugar turns golden. Remove from the heat and gently stir in a small batch of the choux buns to lightly coat them with sugar syrup. Quickly and carefully remove with two metal spoons and transfer to the cone, arranging them as carefully as possible to give a good shape. Continue with the remaining choux buns to fill the cone; reserve a few to fill in any gaps later.

5 Invert the cone on to a serving plate and set aside to harden (this takes about 15 minutes). Peel off cone and foil. Dip the reserved choux buns in warm caramel and add to the cone to make a perfect shape. Decorate with gold and silver dragées or almonds and serve within a few hours.

• Pack choux buns into freezer bags and freeze for up to 1 month. Defrost, then crisp in oven for 5–6 minutes.

Opposite: *Croquembouche (left) and Orange and raspberry trifle (recipe on page 97)*

CHAPTER FOUR

christmas cakes

Christmas without cake is almost unthinkable, but you don't have to plump for the traditional rough snow scene. You will have great fun making the iced cakes here: the Father Christmas one is charming and fun, and the elegant Festive flowers cake is really pretty. The other cakes in this chapter are quick and simple but equally delicious – some of them can be made in advance and frozen, leaving you plenty of time to join the party!

North Pole

Tiers aren't just for wedding cakes. These two Christmas designs will feed any number of family and guests – or just make the top if you don't need so much. They may take a bit of time, but I'm sure you'll agree, the stunning results make it worthwhile.

the icing on the cake

Father Christmas cake

YOU WILL NEED

1 x 15 and 25cm/6 and 10in round rich fruit cakes • **15cm/6in round cake card** • 40cm/16in round drum cake board • **2 tbsp apricot jam, warmed and sieved** • icing sugar, for dusting • **2kg/4½ lb marzipan** • 2.5kg/5½ lb white ready-to-roll icing • **blue, green, orange, brown, red, yellow and black paste food colours and artist's paint brush** • 2 rounded tbsp royal icing and snow glitter • **15cm/6in bamboo skewer** • piping bag and no 1 plain piping nozzle

1 Place the 15cm/6in cake on the cake card and the 25cm/10in cake in the centre of the cake board, then brush both cakes with warm apricot jam.

2 Lightly dust a work surface with icing sugar. Knead and roll out one-third of the marzipan to 3mm/⅛in thick and drape over the small cake. Roll out the remaining marzipan and cover the large cake. Smooth over the top and sides with the palm of your hand, or use a cake icing smoother if you have one. Trim the edges and leave to dry for 24 – 48 hours.

3 When the marzipan is dry, bring a little water to the boil, leave to go cold, then brush lightly over each cake. Colour 1.8kg/4lb of ready-to-roll icing pale blue, then roll out on a work surface lightly dusted with icing sugar. Cover both cakes, smooth over top and sides, then trim. Reserve the trimmings for decoration.

4 Place the small cake on top of the large cake, centred. Using 225g/8oz of white icing, thinly roll out a 7.5cm/3in wide strip to go round the base of the cake board. Lightly dampen the board and position the strip. Reserve trimmings for decoration.

North Pole
129,761
miles

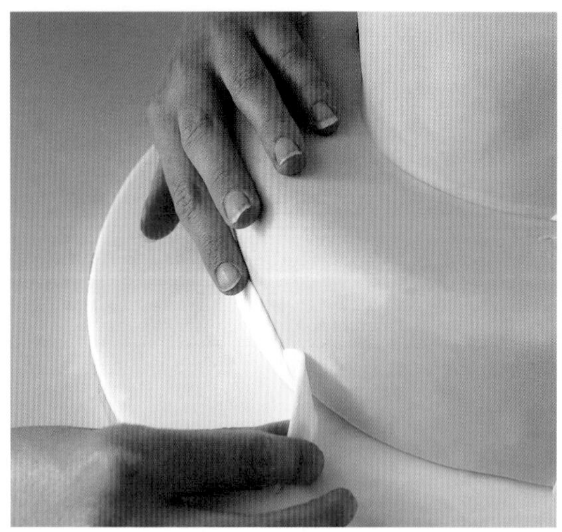

5 Thinly roll out 100g/4oz of white icing and cut out different height 'hills'. Stick around the base of each cake with a little water. Roll out a rough circle using 50g/2oz white icing and stick to the top of the cake with water. Using a palette knife, spread a little royal icing randomly around the board and on the top cake. Stipple with a damp pastry brush, sprinkle with glitter.

6 Colour 175g/6oz icing dark green for the fir trees. Make various size cones and flatten each one slightly. Using scissors, snip each cone to create branches, brush with royal icing and dust with glitter. Stick to the sides of the cake with water.

7 **Make eight snowmen:** flatten two small balls of white icing for each body. Colour tiny amounts of icing for the scarves, then roll out thinly. Colour tiny cones orange for 'carrot' noses and a little icing, pale brown for hats. Stick together with water and position around cake.

8 **Make the signpost:** roll out a tiny piece of white icing and cut out a sign. Roll out a thin sausage of white icing and insert the bamboo skewer. Leave both to dry overnight.

9 **Make Santa:** colour and shape pieces as shown (right), then stick together with water. Cut out a piece of white icing for the present list. Colour remaining icing to make a teddy, Santa's sack and presents. Pipe the ribbons and bows using coloured royal icing (below).

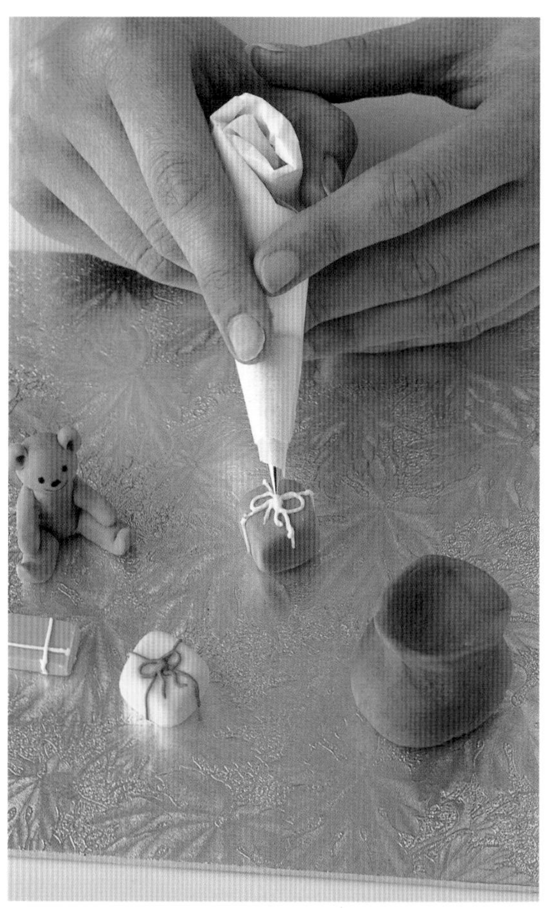

10 **Place Santa on the cake:** using black food colour, paint on the facial features of Santa and teddy, the snowmen's eyes, the North Pole signpost lettering and the list. Stick the signpost together with water and push into the cake, then position the present list. Pipe on Santa's eyebrows, the 'fur' trim around his coat, boots, wrists and hat, plus the belt buckle if not already done. Pipe royal icing on the signpost to give the effect of snow, and tiny dots over both cakes.

Festive flowers cake

YOU WILL NEED

1 x 15 and 25cm/6 and 10in round rich fruit cakes • **15cm/6in round cake card** • 40cm/16in round drum cake board • **2 tbsp apricot jam, warmed and sieved** • icing sugar, for dusting • **2kg/4½lb marzipan** • 2kg/4½lb white ready-to-roll icing • **115g/4oz royal icing – 55g/2oz left white and 25g/1oz each coloured green and red** • snow glitter • **135g/4¾oz petal paste – 40g/1½oz white, 20g/¾oz each of pale golden yellow and ivory and 50g/2oz dark green** • small, medium and large holly cutters • **small, medium and large ivy leaf cutters** • rounded modelling tool • **artist's fine paint brush** • green paste food colour • **wooden skewer** • gold and yellow dusting powders • **piping bag and no 2 plain nozzle** • yellow stamens

1 Place the 15cm/6in cake on the cake card and the 25cm/10in cake in the centre of the cake board, then brush both cakes with warm apricot jam.

2 Lightly dust a work surface with icing sugar. Knead and roll out one-third of the marzipan to 3mm/⅛in thick and drape over the small cake. Roll out the remaining marzipan and cover the larger cake. Smooth over the top and sides with the palm of your hand, or use a cake icing smoother if you have one. Trim the edges and leave to dry for 24 – 48 hours.

3 When the marzipan on both cakes is dry, bring a little water to the boil, leave to go cold, then brush lightly over the marzipan on each cake. Cover both cakes using 1.8kg/4lb white icing and smooth over the top and sides. Trim any excess. Place the small cake on top of the large one, centred. Using 225g/8oz white icing, thinly roll out a 7.5cm/3in wide strip to go round the base of the cake board. Lightly dampen the board and position the strip. Using a palette knife, spread a little royal icing randomly around the board and the top of the cakes. Stipple the icing with a damp pastry brush, then sprinkle with glitter.

4 **Make the holly and ivy:** thinly roll out 20g/¾oz of dark green petal paste for the holly, a little at a time. Using different size cutters, cut out lots of leaves. Soften the edges of each leaf on the palm of your hand, using the modelling tool. Leave to dry overnight, then lightly steam over the spout of a boiling kettle to give them a sheen. Make the ivy: thinly roll out the ivory petal paste, a little at a time. Using different size cutters, cut out lots of leaves. Leave to dry overnight, then paint centres with green food colour (right).

5 **Make the snowdrop leaves:** thinly roll out the remaining dark green paste and cut out the long, tapering leaves with a sharp knife. Score the centre of the leaves with the point of the knife and then leave to dry overnight (left).

6 Make the winter aconite (A): using the pale yellow petal paste, form a small ball of paste into a cone. Hollow out the centre with pointed end of the skewer and cut into six equal petals. Pull and flatten each petal using your fingers and shape to a point. Leave to dry, then dust with gold dusting powder. Pipe a small dot of royal icing into the centre of each flower and stick in the stamens.

7 Make the Christmas roses (B): use white petal paste and make in the same way as the aconite. Cut into five equal petals. Shape the petals and soften each one with the modelling tool. When dry, dust the centre lightly with yellow powder, paint centre green, then pipe yellow dots of icing.

8 Make the snowdrops (C): take a tiny pinch of white petal paste and make a cone. Hollow out the centre with a wooden skewer. Make a slightly larger cone, and hollow out in the same way. Cut the large cone into three even petals. Thin and shape the petals with your fingers. Dampen the centre and stick the smaller cone inside the larger one. When dry, paint the inside with a little green food colouring.

9 Use the dark green royal icing to pipe stems for the snowdrops and winter aconite (above). Position the flower heads and stick in place with royal icing. Attach the ivy and snowdrop leaves, sticking in place with a little water (left). Arrange holly leaves in small sprigs and secure with water. Pipe in berries using the red royal icing, then use royal icing to secure and position the Christmas roses.

There will be times during the Christmas season when you will want to serve a cake that does not take hours to make and is not too rich and heavy. These Big Easy Christmas cakes are designed with this in mind – all of them can be thrown together quickly, or made in advance and frozen until needed. They all taste and look just as good as any traditional Christmas cake, and your family and friends will be glad to try out something a little different.

the big easy christmas cakes

Mincemeat, apple and marzipan strudel

Serves 6 – 8

350g/12oz mincemeat
2 eating apples, peeled, cored and grated
175g/6oz marzipan, chopped
6 sheets filo pastry, thawed if frozen
25g/1oz butter, melted
icing sugar, for dusting

1 Preheat oven to 200°C/400°C/Gas 6. Mix mincemeat, apples and marzipan. Place two sheets of pastry, slightly overlapping, on a greased baking sheet. Brush with butter and place two more sheets on top, brush with butter and cover with remaining pastry.
2 Spread the mincemeat along one long pastry edge to within 2.5cm/1in of the ends. Fold in the ends and roll up the pastry loosely. Brush with the remaining butter. Mark several times with a sharp knife.
3 Bake for 30 – 35 minutes until the pastry is golden. Dust with icing sugar and serve warm.

• The strudel can be frozen for up to 1 month.

Rich Christmas log

This rich and creamy orange liqueur log should be served in small portions. Once decorated, freeze until solid, then wrap in freezer film. Unwrap before thawing overnight in the fridge and dusting with cocoa powder.

Serves 14

4 eggs
100g/4oz caster sugar
75g/3oz plain flour
25g/1oz cocoa powder

FOR THE SYRUP

50g/2oz caster sugar
4 tbsp Cointreau or orange flavoured liqueur

TO DECORATE

450ml/¾ pint double cream
200g/7oz white chocolate, broken into small pieces
grated rind of 1 orange
3 tbsp Cointreau or orange flavoured liqueur
200g/7oz plain chocolate, broken into small pieces
coarse Chocolate caraque (recipe opposite)
cocoa powder, for dusting (optional)

1 Preheat the oven to 200°C/400°F/Gas 6. Grease and line a 33 x 23cm/13 x 9in Swiss roll tin. Whisk the eggs and sugar in a bowl, set over a pan of simmering water, until the mixture leaves a trail when the whisk is lifted. Remove from the heat and whisk until cool.

2 Sift the flour and cocoa powder over the bowl and fold in using a large metal spoon. Turn into the tin, easing into the corners. Bake for 15 minutes or until firm to touch. Sprinkle a clean sheet of greaseproof with a little caster sugar and invert the sponge on to it. Peel away the lining paper. Roll up the sponge from the long side and leave to cool.

3 Make the syrup: heat the sugar in a small pan with 150ml/¼ pint water until the sugar dissolves. Boil for 2 minutes until syrupy. Stir in the liqueur and leave to cool.

4 Bring 150ml/¼ pint of cream almost to the boil in a small pan. Remove from the heat and stir in the white chocolate until melted, then stir in the orange rind and liqueur and leave to cool. Bring the remaining cream almost to the boil and stir in the plain chocolate. Leave until melted; stir and set aside to cool.

5 Gently unroll the sponge and sprinkle with the syrup. Lightly whisk the white chocolate mixture until just holding its shape and spread over the sponge. Roll up the sponge and cut off a quarter of the roll, diagonally. Place the sponge on a plate (or flat tray if freezing) and position the cut portion against one side. Lightly whisk the plain chocolate cream until holding its shape. Spread over the sponge. Decorate with chocolate caraque and dust with cocoa powder, if liked.

Chocolate caraque

Melt 200g/7oz plain chocolate with 15g/½ oz unsalted butter and spread on to a marble slab, clean baking sheet or work surface. Leave until set but not brittle. Draw a knife across at a 45° angle. The knife angle affects the tightness of the chocolate curls.

Light tropical fruit cake

This colourful, fruit-glazed cake has a lovely moist texture and is much lighter than a traditional rich fruit Christmas cake. After cooking, wrap loosely and freeze in a rigid container. Glaze and scatter with the cherries and coconut once thawed.

Serves 16

675g/1½lb mixed dried tropical fruits such as papaya, mango, pineapple
100g/4oz dried apricots
100/4oz sultanas
85ml/3fl oz brandy
200g/7oz unsalted butter, softened
200g/7oz caster sugar
3 eggs, beaten
200g/7oz plain flour
1 tsp baking powder
2 tsp vanilla essence
40g/1½oz desiccated coconut
75g/3oz brazil nuts, roughly chopped
75g/3oz hazelnuts, roughly chopped
25g/1oz crystallized or glacé ginger
1 tbsp pumpkin seeds

TO DECORATE

25g/1oz multi-coloured glacé cherries, chopped
4 tbsp clear honey
toasted fresh coconut shavings

1 Process 400g/14oz of the mixed tropical fruits in a food processor with the apricots until chopped into small pieces. Transfer to a bowl and add the sultanas and brandy. Cover and leave for 3 hours or overnight.

2 Preheat the oven to 150°C/300°F/Gas 2. Grease and line a 20cm/8in round cake tin. Beat together the butter and sugar until creamy, then gradually beat in the eggs, adding a little of the flour to prevent curdling.

3 Sift the remaining flour and the baking powder into the bowl and stir in. Add the vanilla essence, coconut, 50g/2oz each of the nuts, the ginger and brandy-steeped fruits. Turn into the tin and level the surface.

4 Lightly process the remaining tropical fruits so they remain chunky and scatter over the cake with the remaining nuts and the pumpkin seeds. Place the cake in the oven and reduce the temperature to 140°C/275°F/Gas 1. Bake for 2½ hours or until a skewer, inserted into the centre, comes out clean. Cool in the tin.

5 Scatter over the cherries, brush with honey, then sprinkle with the coconut shavings.

Truffle torte

Serves 10 – 12

For the chocolate sponge base

75g/3oz soft margarine
75g/3oz caster sugar
2 medium eggs
50g/2oz self-raising flour, sifted
25g/1oz cocoa powder, sifted

For the truffle mix

75g/3oz glucose
75g/3oz caster sugar
85ml/3fl oz water
4 leaves gelatine, soaked
450g/1lb dark chocolate, melted over a double boiler
600ml/1 pint double cream, semi-whipped
225g/8oz jar of cherries in liqueur (or any soft fruits preserved in alcohol)

To decorate

150ml/¼ pint whipping cream, whipped
225g/8oz white chocolate, melted
icing sugar

1 Make the chocolate sponge: preheat the oven to 180°C/350°F/Gas 4. Grease and flour an 18cm/7in round sandwich tin. Cream the margarine and sugar until light and fluffy. Beat in the eggs, one at a time. Fold in the sifted flour and cocoa powder. Place mixture into the sandwich tin and bake for 20 minutes until springy to the touch. Turn out on to a cooling rack.

2 Make the truffle mix: mix together the glucose, caster sugar and water in a small pan and heat until dissolved. Add the soaked gelatine and allow to cool to luke warm. Add to the melted chocolate, then fold in the semi-whipped cream.

3 Assemble the cake: place your chocolate sponge into a deep 20cm/8in round loose-bottomed cake tin, and pour over the syrup from the jar of fruit. Place the fruit on top, then spoon on the truffle mix and level off. Place in the fridge to set. Pipe on the whipped cream to form a dome in the middle.

4 Make the rose: meanwhile, place a baking tray into the freezer and leave it for at least 1 hour. Pour a small amount of the melted white chocolate on to the tray and, using a palette knife, spread very thinly.

5 When set, cut into strips – these do not have to be uniform in any way; you could have curvy lines,

straight lines and different lengths. Remove strips from tray with the aid of a palette knife. Continue with the remaining chocolate. Starting from the centre of the cake, place the white chocolate strips, standing upright on their sides, on to the cream, building up layers to make a rose shape to cover the entire cake. Dust with icing sugar.

Penguin snowball cake

This charming little fellow will delight the children, and the no-bake cake mixture is so easy that the kids can also make it themselves. Omit the rum if you are making the penguins for children!

Makes 3 penguins

FOR THE TROPICAL CHOCOLATE CRUNCH CAKE

50g/2oz glacé cherries
50g/2oz raisins
175g/6oz dried pineapple, peach, pear and apricot chopped
50ml/2fl oz rum
175g/6oz dark chocolate
100g/4oz butter
300ml/10fl oz condensed milk
225g/8oz digestive biscuits, broken

FOR THE ICING

Make up approximately 900g/2lb royal icing:
2 egg whites
750g/1lb 8oz icing sugar, sifted
juice of 1/2 lemon

FOR THE PENGUINS

100g/4oz black roll-out icing
50g/2oz orange roll-out icing
25g/1oz white roll-out icing

1 Make the tropical chocolate crunch: soak the dried fruits in the rum for at least 2 hours, but preferably overnight. Place the chocolate, butter and condensed milk into a saucepan and heat over a low heat, stirring all the time, until it is all melted. Bring to the boil, then remove from the heat. Stir in the broken biscuits and fruits, leave to cool and then divide into 3 balls. Place in the fridge to set (takes around 2 hours).

2 Make the royal icing coating: using a fork, break up the egg whites, then gradually beat in the icing sugar. Stir in the lemon juice and continue beating in the icing sugar until the mixture forms soft peaks. Coat each ball of tropical chocolate crunch with royal icing and, using a palette knife, make soft peaks and swirls with the icing all over the ball. Use the remaining icing to coat a 30cm/12in round cake board.

3 Make the penguins: place the 3 iced balls on the cake board (do not leave the icing to set) – these are the penguins' bodies. Set aside a tiny amount of the black icing for the penguins' eyes. Divide the remainder of the black icing into 4 equal parts. Roll 3 of the parts into round balls for the penguins' heads. Use the remaining parts to make the 6 wings. Divide the orange icing into 9, 3 parts for the penguins' beaks, and 6 for their feet. Divide the white icing into 6 for the penguins' eyes, and use the tiny amount of black icing set aside earlier for the pupils, sticking them on with a little water. Stick all the parts on to the 'bodies' while the icing is still soft.

Templates

Christmas tree biscuits

p.12

all shown actual size

Christmas tree decorations

p.16

all shown actual size

Goose sack

p.60

enlarge on copier 200%
to get actual size

BEAK

HOLLY LEAF
x 2

HOLLY LEAF
x 6

GOOSE

WING

LEG
x 2

Christmas tree sack

p.63

enlarge on copier 200%
to get actual size

TUB

STAR

TREE

Lay straight edge of enlarged template along folded edge of material

INDEX

CONTRIBUTORS

FEATURES/DESIGNS

Jane Asher: The icing on the cake (cakes made by Susie Spiller and Wendy Mills)

Lorna Brash *(with Gilly Cubitt)****:*** Edible presents (Brown sugar meringues, Mixed nut pralines, Lebkuchen, Moroccan preserved lemons, Cranberry gin)

Sarah Buenfeld: Edible presents (Luxury dark chocolate and Grand marnier truffles)

Mary Cadogan: Christmas drinks party; New Year's Eve supper (with Mitzie Wilson); Big Easy Christmas cakes (Mincemeat, apple and marzipan strudel)

Ruth Clarke: Big Easy Christmas cakes (Penguin snowball cake and Truffle torte)

Gilly Cubitt *(with Lorna Brash)*: Edible presents (Brown sugar meringues, Mixed nut pralines, Lebkuchen, Moroccan preserved lemons, Cranberry gin)

Angela Dukes: Hand-made cards; Gift wrap

Joanna Farrow: Christmas Eve supper; Big Easy Christmas cakes (Rich Christmas log and Light tropical fruit cake)

Bridget Hetzel: Beautiful crackers; Christmas sacks (feature)

Caroline Kelley: Tree decorations; Decorations around the home; Gift wrap (Ivy leaf print only); Gift tags; Table decorations (not Medieval table decorations); Hand-made cards (Music card, Embossed card, Wreath card and Leaf card only); Christmas sacks (design)

Janice Murfitt: Edible presents (Mini gingerbread houses, Amaretti, Novelty ginger biscuits, Gingerbread window biscuits)

Angela Nilsen: Tree decorations

Sue Russell: Medieval table decorations

Andrea Spencer: Tree decorations; Decorations around the home; Gift wrap (Ivy leaf print only; Gift tags; Table decorations (not Medieval table decorations); Hand-made cards (Wreath card and Leaf card only)

Helen Trent: Mantelpiece ideas

Stuart Walton: Mulled drinks

Mitzie Wilson: New Year's Eve supper (with Mary Cadogan)

HOME ECONOMISTS

Joanna Farrow: Christmas Eve supper

Kerenza Harries: Big Easy Christmas cakes (Mincemeat, apple and marzipan strudel)

Jane Lawrie: New Year's Eve supper

Pete Smith: Christmas drinks paarty

Sunil Vijayakar: Big Easy Christmas cakes (Rich Christmas log and Light tropical fruit cake)

PHOTOGRAPHERS

William Adams-Lingwood: Beautiful crackers (step-by-step photographs), Edible presents (Mini gingerbread houses, Amaretti, Novelty ginger biscuits, Gingerbread window biscuits)

Robin Broadbent: Mulled drinks

Paul Bricknell: The holly and the ivy; Big Easy Christmas cakes (Penguin snowball cake and Truffle torte)

Martin Brigdale: Mantelpiece ideas (Silver sophistication and Children's fireplace)

Simon Butcher: Christmas sacks (step-by-step photographs only)

Jean Cazals: Luxury dark chocolate and Grand Marnier truffles; Christmas Eve supper

Angela Dukes: Hand-made cards

Ken Field: Mantelpiece ideas (Golden glow and Tinsel town); Medieval table decorations; Beautiful crackers (cracker photographs); Gift wrap (except Ivy leaf print); Christmas sacks (main photographs); Edible presents (Brown sugar meringues, Mixed nut pralines, Lebkuchen, Moroccan preserved lemons, Cranberry gin); Big Easy Christmas cakes (Rich Christmas log and Light tropical fruit cake); The icing on the cake

Gus Filgate: New Year's Eve supper

James Murphy: Big Easy Christmas cakes (Mincemeat, apple and marzipan strudel)

Alan Olley: Jacket photograph; Decorations (chapter opener); Cards and gifts (chapter opener)

Spike Powell: Tree decorations; Decorations around the home; Gift wrap (Ivy leaf print only); Gift tags; Table decorations (not Medieval table decorations); Hand-made cards (Wreath card only)

Roger Stowell: Christmas drinks party

STYLISTS

Angela Dukes: Gift wrap (except Ivy leaf print); Edible presents (Mini gingerbread houses, Amaretti, Novelty ginger biscuits, Gingerbread window biscuits)

Penny Markham: New Year's Eve supper

Helen Payne: Big Easy Christmas cakes (Mincemeat, apple and marzipan strudel)

Sue Russell: Medieval table decorations; Christmas Eve supper

Andrea Spencer: Tree decorations; Decorations around the home; Gift wrap (Ivy leaf print only); Gift tags; Table decorations (not Medieval table decorations); Hand-made cards (Music card, Embossed card, Wreath card and Leaf card only)

Helen Trent: Mantelpiece ideas; Beautiful crackers; Luxury dark chocolate and Grand Marnier truffles; Christmas drinks party; Big Easy Christmas cakes (Rich Christmas log and Light tropical fruit cake)

Judy Williams: Edible presents (Brown sugar meringues, Mixed nut pralines, Lebkuchen, Moroccan preserved lemons, Cranberry gin)